# Considerations

## A Guide for Moving Abroad

# Queen D. Michele

# Dedication

To my son, Thaddeus N. Williams II,
and my daughter, Deonna M. Solano

*I did something while I was here*

# Acknowledgements

The Ladies
Wine & Wisdom
The Solange
Dr. Frantonia Pollins *planted the seed
Pastor Christina Seastrunk *watered the seed
Sara Kelly Keenan
Lisa Staub

Copyright © Queen D. Michele Ajijic, Mexico.
Edited by Kathy Koches & Nana Anu
First Edition: January 2019
Publisher: Ajijic Books
Cover design: Mike Riley, Queen Michele
Book design: www.ajijicbooks.com

# Contents

# Preface

This book is designed to help the reader contemplate the most essential things to consider when planning and preparing to move abroad. I did it by myself and gathered what I consider to be pertinent information during the process. It is my belief that this information is most beneficial to a certain demographic, as I am a middle-aged, single, retired female. That is a growing demographic and more and more women are pondering the possibility of living abroad for many of the same reasons I did.

I had been retired from teaching elementary school for two years when I woke up one morning with an epiphany; I will *always* have to work. When I first retired and began receiving my pension I quickly realized a supplemental income of sorts would be needed to maintain the standard of living I had while working. Okay, no problem. I was retired and I'd find some fun stuff to do, work my own schedule and earn the cash needed. That's exactly what happened. I first began doing contractual work remotely for an educational software company. My job was to critique lessons already in the company's data base system and then return to the cloud for teachers to pull down and use in their classroom.

I also started driving for Uber/Lyft, I did Postmates, Merchandising, and Secret Shopping. I was having a ball, especially because I was someone who had been regulated by bells for 27 years. As a teacher there was a bell to start the day, a bell to eat lunch, and a bell to end the day, along with all the other bells, classroom intercom interruptions, fire drills, and shelter in places. I was making my own schedule, meeting fascinating people, doing things I had never done before and all the while making the supplemental money to stay afloat. My all-time favorite job was working as a shuttle driver for a transportation company that serviced the railroad. My job was to transport engineers and conductors to and from their trains. Trains arrived on and off site of the railyard. I was a yard driver and it was the coolest job ever! I had so much fun cutting up with the guys and a few women too. When I wasn't picking anyone up, I was parked under a tree reading, playing games, talking on the phone, listening to music and watching TV. Now as much as I loved that gig, it wasn't what I intended to do for years to come to sustain myself. So, it happened that a new CEO took over the railroad company and with his new reign came many changes. One such change was cutting back on yard drivers. Fortunately, when the axe came down I had already had my epiphany and was executing small moves positioning myself to move abroad.

The considerations I write about in this book are specific to moving to Mexico. However, I believe these considerations are relative to any country when you are planning and preparing to move abroad. There is research to be done, resources to gather, videos to watch, and articles to read. It becomes wonderfully all-consuming and you'll love it. It makes you happy, and (you know... that you know... that you know) you're really going to do it. You decide your path, pin it and announce to the world. At least that's what I did, and the journey began.

This book is a practical guide that illuminates the most important considerations needed to execute a calculated move abroad. If I did it, you can too. It was never my intention to write a book about how I moved abroad as a single, middle-aged retiree, yet, I've come to realize this book is purposeful and I am over the moon delighted to positively contribute to your journey. I wish for you to find that happy place abroad, as I have, and to go about this next chapter of your life intentionally living your highest good.

# Chapter One

# Consider: Faith vs Fear

To have an undoubtedly impenetrable belief in something or someone when verification is not present through the senses is what it means to have faith. One can't see it, hear it, taste it, smell it or touch it. Nevertheless, having faith means that something or someone does exist, or is going to happen. On the other hand, the word fear or afraid carries the opposite meaning. The words fear and afraid can be used interchangeably because their meanings are very similar. For example, I could say **I fear** or I'm **afraid**. Both words mean:

- to feel anxiety or apprehension on behalf of
- to worry that something undesirable will occur or be
- unwilling or reluctant to do something for fear of the consequences
- to be frightened
- afraid of someone or something that is likely to be dangerous,
- painful or threatening

Based on the above list, it appears fear can and does take a firm crippling grip on a person's psyche. Fear has been known to even paralyze a person's movement. I doubt very seriously if anyone wants to build more anxiety, apprehension, and reluctance into their lives. If you're considering moving abroad but your fear is bigger than your faith, the question then becomes how do you build your faith, so you can begin planning and preparing for such a move?

I submit to you what worked for me, although I've never really been a fearful person. However, whenever I was contemplating a big change in my life and fear rose within my thought life, I visualized. Simply put, seeing is believing, and faith is the byproduct of belief. Visualization is a powerful tool I use to help combat fear and shift the negative vibrations I'm putting out. I believe what you put your attention or thoughts on creates the vibrations (energy) that emit from your very being. Have you ever observed how a person can walk into a room and change the entire atmosphere of that room based on the energy that's being emitted from them? Have you ever caught good or bad vibes from someone in or around your personal space? The Universe doesn't know if the vibrations/energy a person emits or puts out is because of what is being imagined/visualized, or what is being observed. In either case, it (the Universe) is responding to that vibration.

Once I got a clear understanding of how powerful visualizing is and how to use it effectively it grew my faith, diminished my fears, and propelled me into taking leaps of faith in my life. Moving from Detroit to Las Vegas with an 8-year-old and an 11-year-old, not knowing anyone, was a leap of faith. Moving to Atlanta from Las Vegas without securing employment beforehand was a leap of faith. I know that the mind is a battlefield where thoughts war against each other. Visualizing is my most effective weapon to use on that battlefield. Sometimes, negative visualizations can work in the opposite way and promote fear. However, the visuals that create fear worked as a positive in my case, which propelled me into action.

I feared always having to work to supplement my pension until my mind and body wouldn't let me anymore. I feared having to live sub-standardly because of what it would cost me for healthcare insurance. I feared being a burden on my kids. I began visualizing being 70 years old saying, "Welcome to Walmart." We've all seem them in our local neighborhoods, super markets, restaurants, movie theaters and airports. Middle-aged women bagging, cashiering, taking orders and greeting. Those visions and the fear it brought into to my thought life set in motion my biggest leap of faith ever.

The Universe is perfect. What I needed, when I needed it, presented itself to me, as I believe it will for you. Something, someone, some event, book, video or sermon will make its way into your path and your paradigm will shift.

It happened for me through a magazine article. While living in fear and visualizing the worst-case scenarios for myself I came across an in-depth article in "International Living; The Top Ten Places to Retire." I began researching and visualizing myself living in the places listed. During that process my faith began to grow by leaps and bounds. It is said that one can overcome fear thoughts with its opposite, faith thoughts. I had been researching and visualizing for a few months when I made this Facebook post. Notice the hash tag fearless.

**Queen D. Michele October 26, 2016, 11:10am**

"Strongly considering retiring/living abroad within the next three years; Peru, Belize, Costa Rica, Panama, Mexico or possibly going home to the Mother Land. Definitely have started my research. The possibilities excite me." #gypsy #travel #I can do anything #**fearless** #one life to live #expat

18 Days Later another post

**Queen D. Michele. November 13, 2016, 11:45pm.**

"The decision has been made, planned out (pretty much to a "T") and written down. In the fall of 2018 or possibly sooner, I'll arrive in one of the quaint towns near Lake Chapala in Jalisco, Mexico. I'm immersing myself in all things relating to living abroad; forums, blogs, groups, videos, and mastering Spanish with courses and apps throughout this next year."

I'll be 55 years old when I move.

* TESOL endorsed (may do a little part time ESL teaching)
* living comfortably on my retirement
* own car
* fluent in Spanish
* healthy and free

If God willing, and the creek don't rise.

When I made that post the research was over and my faith was on steroids. Any fear about moving abroad alone was gone. I was fully persuaded about and committed to the move. I made that post knowing full well that people would hold me accountable for what I said, and I wanted to be held accountable. Hell I announced it on Facebook as I would an engagement, marriage, new relationship status, birth, death, graduation or any other important event. Once the announcement had been made I started taking notes on the how, when and where of the move. Those notes were my start. Having held on to them, I'm referring to them now as I write.

A few, but not all the things I starred within my post, materialized. You, like me will notice as you continue to visualize yourself living abroad that certain plans will inevitably change. For instance, I never became TESOL endorsed to teach English. Initially, I strongly entertained the idea of applying for the International Teacher Training Organization (ITTO), a four-week accredited certification program. The courses taken during the four weeks would help me teach English as a Foreign or Second Language effectively. The school is situated in Guadalajara, MX which is 30 minutes from the Lakeside area where I was planning to live. Guadalajara is the second biggest city in Mexico. The school offered a few options for boarding accommodations while completing the course. The option I contemplated was living with a host family. The home I would live in for a month would be a short bus ride to the school. At that time my thinking was to totally submerge myself in the culture and language of the country. Other choices were hostels, four and five-star hotels, and furnished apartments. Those accommodations were within walking distance to the school and all with varying prices.

As I continued researching, planning and preparing **I realized** that I really didn't have a desire to teach anymore. I was, in fact, retired and I wanted to live as such. The other determining factor was that the pay is extremely low. Committing to low pay and long hours felt asinine, so that idea was scrapped.

You'll find other plans will get recalculated. I was 54 instead of 55 when I moved, and my departure date was pushed up to December 1, 2017 instead of the fall of 2018. Also, I'm nowhere near fluent in Spanish. During my time planning and preparing I signed up for a Spanish class on line. I received a good deal through Groupon. I still have and use that course which focuses mainly on grammar. I downloaded Duolingo, a language app from my play store. Duolingo's main concentration is vocabulary and it uses a gaming format to engage the user. It's a pretty cool app and challenging at the same time. Finally, as it relates to learning Spanish, my niece e-mailed me the entire Pimsleur series which is comparable to Rosetta Stone and focuses on pronunciation and reading. Yet, with the grammar, vocabulary and speaking practices in place and being consistently used, **I realized** that speaking fluently is going to take quite some time.

I didn't bring my car. My initial plan was to pay off my 2007 Chevy Colbalt, pack it, attach a mini trailer to the back and take my car with me. Research proved however, with that plan there was much to consider (More on transportation in Chapter 7). The ends and outs of border crossing, itemized lists, permits, costs and nationalizing time frames once across the border depending on your visa led me to scrap that idea too.

Wonderful climate, the ability to live comfortably on my pension, closeness to the United States, and an active retirement lifestyle was what I was looking for as I began researching moving abroad. Mexico was not my first choice. I was looking at Costa Rica. My daughter's husband is Costa Rican. His mother and father still frequently visit the country and have family there. I came across a young black couple's YouTube channel who were living there and vlogging about their experiences. The surroundings were beautiful and like Mexico, fresh fruits, meats, and vegetables are readily available. It just felt too rural for my taste. It didn't resonate with me and I didn't see myself doing or being involved with too much of anything. I remember Belize's visa requirements being too expensive, and there were too many hoops to jump through. I looked at South Africa and West Africa as well. It was expensive in most of the areas that I researched. There were big beautiful buildings within the city with lots of congested streets. Any possible middle ground was pricey or just about to begin development. Colombia is exploding with millennials. It's a hot travel destination spot for them. It has everything for the up and coming progressive, sort of like Dubai. I scanned over Nicaragua, Panama, and Ecuador but none of those countries really resonated with me.

The region where I chose to live in Mexico had all the criteria I was looking for during my initial research. The climate in Lakeside is marvelous (the days are warm and sunny with an average of 75 degrees), I can live comfortably on my pension, it's close to my home base (3 1/2-hour plane ride), and it has a large active expat community. Mexico has 32 states. I live in the state of Jalisco. This state houses the largest lake in the country. It's called Lake Chapala. Situated around this massive lake are quaint little towns, villages and beautiful mountains. Each town has a town square or plaza with a Catholic Church at its center. Most have a malecon, a paved public walkway, off the lake with restaurants, bars, shops, playgrounds, and picnic areas. What a malecon entails depends on the town or village. Some have large malecons and squares and others are small. I live on the north side of the lake, situated between the municipal town of Chapala, and the major hub of the expat community, the village of Ajijic. Both are very short bus rides to the left or right depending on what side of the street I'm standing on, and I know many residents that walk from our town, San Antonio Tlayacapan, to Ajijic. I've only done it once since living here. Needless to say, I don't need a car. I either walk, take a bus, ride with a friend or call a personal driver. Transportation is never a problem.

An active retired lifestyle is very important to me. I want to enjoy many different adventures. It was never my intent to just sit down and become a couch potato. During my research, I was drawn to Mexico and the Lakeside area in particular because of the many activities I saw available to retirees. A major springboard for activity here is a place called Lake Chapala Society (LCS). It serves pretty much as the expat headquarters, located in Ajijic. LCS wasn't always located in the village however. Its history dates back to early 1955 when a small group of foreign residents formed a society inviting all foreign residents of Chapala to join. It was located in Chapala and called Chapala Society. Foreign residents and the local community both benefited from the venture.   In 1983 Neill James agreed to rent the front portion of her estate in Ajijic to the Society. She died at almost 100 years old in 1994. The name was changed to the Lake Chapala Society and it has grown into what it is today, which is a place with a beautiful campus bustling with all types of programs, classes, publications, bus trips, health fairs, a library, postal services, and much more, including an expat directory.

Everything is laid out for the newcomer. The campus is lovely with ponds and plant life throughout. During my research, I didn't see any other country embracing retirees with such an inviting and active expat community. I felt I would be able to easily find my tribe amongst a community of people with the same like-mindedness about retirement and living abroad.

**Consider your thought life as you begin planning and preparing to live abroad.** What kind of thoughts consume you? Are your thoughts "faith thoughts" accompanied by faith visualizations? Or are they "fear thoughts" accompanied by fear visualizations?  It doesn't cost you anything to spend some time visualizing your future in another country, enjoying life and traveling a road of self-discovery that you never knew existed. It all starts with a thought, be it positive (faith) or negative (fear). The choice is truly yours, and yours alone. What type of lifestyle do you see yourself living? How active do you want to be? How far is too far from your family? Those questions and many more must be given great consideration. The things that did materialize from my starred list were the absolute best. I am indeed living comfortably on my retirement. Also, the feeling of being free from the stress and low vibrations of the US is very real and I wake up every morning with a smile on my face, and joy in heart. I'm in the best shape I've ever been in since my pre 40's. I hike twice a week and do yoga three times a week. I lost over 20 pounds in the first five months of arriving here and have kept it off. I found an inner circle of friends (my tribe). It was indeed the best decision I could have ever made for myself.

# Chapter Two

## Consider: Finances

My finances, or lack thereof, were the major determining factor in my decision to move abroad. In this chapter I give insight as to how I managed to move abroad and live comfortably on $1,100 dollars a month.

I started my teaching career in 1988, for the Archdiocese of Detroit. I taught second grade at a private Catholic school for two years. The next eight years were spent teaching with the Detroit Public School District. The following four years I spent administrating for two separate charter school entities. In 2002, I relocated to Las Vegas, NV and stepped back into the classroom for another 11 years. I retired in Atlanta, GA after teaching two years, one in Henry County and my last year in Clayton County. My career in education totals 27 years. I like even numbers and it was my initial plan when I moved to Georgia in 2013 to work five more years and retire at the age of 55 with 30 years in education. But at 52 years of age, I retired.

I had a total of 15 years in Detroit, but only nine of them counted toward a pension. My little stints with the Archdiocese of Detroit and administrating within the charter school systems would be included as part of my social security benefits only. My eight-year pension however, was frozen at around $67,000 and waiting on me to claim at the **proper** retirement age to receive a monthly check for the duration of my life. That check was estimating to be around $800 a month **if** I waited. However, once I retired, I decided to withdraw the frozen pension money from Detroit with penalty and place it in an IRA in Georgia where I was living. The monthly pension I receive to date is from my time teaching in Nevada, not Detroit. However, having drawn on Nevada's pension early, I was again penalized. Nevertheless, I'll receive that small monthly check for the duration of my life.

When I first retired in 2015, it quickly became apparent that my pension was going to cover the rent, and the rent only. There was still the car note, insurance, cell phone, electricity, gas, water, trash, cable and grocery bills to cover monthly.

At the very start of retirement, I was fortunate to land a job that allowed me to work from home. I worked for a software company as a curriculum designer. I proofread, edited, and at times added to lessons stored in a huge database, and once cleaned up, sent them back into the cloud for teachers to pull down and use in their classrooms. I was responsible for turning out a specific number of lessons each week. Some lessons were easy and took only twenty minutes, but there were some that took hours to complete. I organized my day so that I would complete half of my workload, take a break and go Uber. After four hours of Uber driving, I would return and complete the other half of the lessons for the day. Although the job paid well, it was contract work, and eventually my contract ended. I had worked as a curriculum designer for almost a year. Since I was already an Uber driver, I also started doing Uber Eats. I was driving people around and delivering food through the app. I enjoyed being an Uber driver and meeting different people from so many different walks of life. Most people were friendly and we struck up interesting conversations. Sometimes I felt like a therapist, I marveled at how people would just opened up, and poured out their life to a complete stranger.

When I needed a break from people, it was cool to just ride with their food, instead of their conversation. I also drove for Lyft and switched between the two apps depending on which one was active with rides. I soon added Postmates to my post retirement repertoire. Postmates is a logistics company that operates through an app much like Uber or Lyft, to deliver not only food but goods. For instance, I received a message to go and purchase a pack of high end black t-shirts from Dillard's. The description, size and quantity were messaged to me. Unlike Uber or Lyft, Postmates mails a credit card to use when purchasing items for their clients. Everything is done through the app, so funds cannot be misappropriated. I delivered the shirts to the penthouse of someone who I believe to have been a professional basketball player. He was extremely tall and had an air about him that said he was used to having people cater to him. Because I don't really follow sports, I didn't recognize him. Most times I received pretty good tips through the Postmates app, but in this particular instance, I remember well because he *didn't* tip, and I was sure he would.

I eventually picked up with retail merchandising as another stream of income. Merchandising is setting up, straightening up, and displaying products in stores in such a way that it stimulates interest and entices customers to make a purchase. This was also contract work. I would log into the database of the company and sign-up for jobs in my area. The company would then send the particulars of that job and a display blueprint of how it was to be set up. I would go to places like Kroger, Walmart, Sam's Club and Target. I'd show my badge, sign in at the service desk, go in the back, pick up what was needed and go about the business of restocking, and refreshing product displays. Afterwards, I would take pictures and download them to the company in order to be paid. It was alright work for a time, being behind the scenes and seeing how things move from the back to the front of stores, was interesting. I also became a Secret Shopper for a time. I Googled the term because it intrigued me, and since I was already out in the streets I thought it would be fun. There are several legitimate mystery shopping companies out there. I did my due diligence in researching the companies before I applied. I liked picking up jobs from the site's database that were food establishments I'd never been to. I would have to pay upfront, but once the receipt was sent in I was reimbursed, plus I was paid for the narrative written on the site. I had to write up a large detailed narrative, answer 25-50 questions, and take photos. A few times, my pay was held up because they wanted more details. Eating at new places in Midtown and Downtown Atlanta was fun, but the work I had to put in after wards was not fun; it was daunting, and I didn't mystery shop for long.

My favorite job was working as a Shuttle Driver for a transportation company that serviced the railroad. It was by far the coolest job I ever had. I hung out at the railyard and waited for calls coming across the radio as I was responsible for taking conductors and engineers to and from their trains. The guys were great, and always had a joke or two during the ride. I learned so much about the railroad and met a couple of great people that I still communicate with today. At some point, I decided to turn one of my bedrooms into an Airbnb for yet another stream of income. Being an Airbnb host was a wonderful experience as well. I met some amazing people.

Once I made the decision to move abroad, I continued to work at the railyard and Uber on my off days. I also continued with my Airbnb room. At the end of May 2017, I stopped driving the shuttle for the railyard because my days and hours were cut dramatically due to the phasing out of drivers for the yard, so it was just a matter of time. Ubering became more of a hassle than a financial benefit around that time. I was getting tired of driving and people getting in and out of my car was starting to irritate me. Not to mention, I had experienced two very small fender benders about three months apart. There was never any damage done to my car, but the insurance fiasco behind both incidents led me to just throw in the towel. I had been Ubering for a little over a year and it served its purpose for a time, but I was done. I started thinking about the fact that I was moving to another country in six months! I needed to focus all my attention on that. So, all things relating to working ceased, except for the Airbnb room which I kept operating until August. For the next five months, I paid my rent, utilities, cell, groceries, gas and miscellaneous from drawing off my Detroit pension that was now situated in a southern credit union. I paid myself one lump sum a month (what I thought would be necessary for me to live) by transferring from my IRA to my regular bank account. I had already begin dipping into my IRA account to help pay for my daughter's upcoming wedding.

In addition, I began paying off large reoccurring monthly bills like my car, cell phone and all the equipment associated with my T-Mobile account. This included all the things cellular companies sell you with the, "We'll just add it on to your monthly bill" for only $2.00 here and $.99 cents there" line. Cell companies tie all things like headsets, bluetooth speakers, tablets, the phone itself, and your actual plan into a nice tight bow around your neck.

Another large reoccurring bill I had was my burial expense policy with Dignity Memorial. I have always told my grown kids that I will not leave them a financial inheritance of any sort when I transition. However, they are not going to have to create a Go-Fund-Me account on Facebook to lay me to rest either. I have financially taken care of my entire memorial package. My kids, basically just need to show up at the chapel for the memorial in Georgia and collect the ashes. Thinking back on my policy, I'm so glad I purchased it and added the transportation and relocation protection plan. My transportation and relocation protection plan states that if I transition while across the border, the company (a separate entity from my policy) will arrange to have me brought back to Georgia.

My financial goal was to move abroad with a $10,000 US cushion, which is roughly $193,000 pesos. I figured with that in savings, along with my monthly pension I could live comfortably. I had researched thoroughly and estimated to the nearest dollar just what my monthly expenses would be. Now, that I am here, I can truly confirm that it is possible to live comfortably as a single person on $1,100 a month in my part of the world. Here is a list of my monthly expenses, in Mexican pesos and in US Dollars.

| Monthly Expenses | Mexican Pesos | US Dollars |
|---|---|---|
| Rent | $ 10,000 | $ 500.00 |
| Gas | $ 300.00 | $ 15.00 |
| Internet/WI FI | $ 389.00 | $ 20.00 |
| Cell | $ 300.00 | $ 15.00 |
| Electric *every other month | $ 136.00 | $ 7.00 |
| Groceries | $ 3,800 | $ 200.00 |
| Entertain't/misc. | $ 2,000 | $ 100.00 |
| Total: | $ 16,925 | $ 857.00 |

My one bedroom, one-bathroom condo, situated in a small gated community, came fully furnished. I have a fireplace, pool and laundry room (2 washers & 2 dyers with free use), and a good view of the lake and mountains from my rooftop. The furnishings on my rooftop, huge plants, table & chairs were also included. Yes, I was really blessed. I absolutely did my due diligence in researching where I wanted to live. I am a single female and feeling safe is my number one priority. Also, since it already came furnished, it was important that I could live with the décor. I don't have a car, so location was also important. I brought my Firestick and pay $8 USD a month for Netflix. That's the extent of my cable. I'm extremely central and can walk or take a short bus ride anywhere I choose to go.

I have two debit cards and one credit card. The credit card is put away and serves only as my health insurance card. I have a debit card with Chase bank in the states and that's where my direct deposit from my pension lands every month. The Capital 360 debit is connected to Chase wherein I can transfer monies and withdraw from a local ATM here. I don't like pulling money from an ATM directly from my Chase debit card because I'm hit twice with fees. Chase charges me $5.00 every time I use an ATM that is not theirs, and that's in additional fee being charged by the ATM itself.

Everyone's financial situation is different for reasons too many to count. Some have never had to "steal from Peter to pay Paul" (it's a figure of speech.) For others, there are 401(k)s, inheritances, homes, savings, investments and insurance policies within their portfolios. Money management has never been a strong characteristic of mine. As a single parent, I was not a saver, I spent most times in financial survival mode. One thing is for certain; having a complete understanding of the way your money will be situated when moving abroad is essential.

**Consider your finances when planning and preparing to live abroad.** Determine for yourself what streams of income you can most assuredly count on. Consider and research thoroughly your monthly expenses in your country of choice. Consider and learn that country's currency and exchange rate compared to the US. Consider paying off large reoccurring bills, such as your car, cell phone and funeral policy. Also, it would be extremely helpful if you download a currency conversion app to use as you learn the currency for the country you live in as the exchange rate fluctuates daily.

Finally, where do you stand on simplicity? I'm presently seven years out before I can claim social security and my Nevada pension is my **only** stream of income. I live a very simple life now that I live abroad. Ask yourself what can or can't you live without, and be honest. Consider that living abroad may not truly be for you. It may sound good in theory, but to put into practice living in a different country, with its different language, culture, food, people and their way of being and doing things is a huge undertaking. If finances, or the lack there of is your only "why" for moving abroad, I'm most certain that you will not have a pleasant experience.

# Chapter Three

# Consider: A Visa

Wherever you move abroad, you most likely will need to obtain a visa. Look at starting your visa process as an adventure; it certainly will be one. In this chapter I will give insight into how I obtained a Residente Permanente Visa. I am still a United States citizen, I just reside in Mexico. I'm known as an expatriate (expat), someone who lives outside their native country. There are several types of visa's one could obtain depending on how they plan to live abroad. Student, work, temporary, and permanent are the basic types of visas I came across during my research. Different countries have different requirements for US citizens attempting to obtain a visa. There are even visa free countries for Americans, and of course research would be necessary to learn of those countries.

The first thing you must have to begin the process is a passport, and from there the adventure begins. I started my visa quest by researching the types of Mexican visas available. I wasn't planning on working or going to school so that left either temporary or permanent. I quickly discovered that your finances will determine the type of visa you will be issued. Countries, at least the ones I researched before settling on Mexico, want to ensure that you don't come into their country and wind up being a financial burden. I settled on getting a temporal visa, based on my $1,100 monthly pension and what I had presently in my IRA. Obtaining a temporal visa was really going to be a stretch for me, especially since my IRA was quickly dwindling down because at the time I using it for living expenses. I had begun using it to tie up loose ends and finance my move. I knew I was going to have to apply for my visa expeditiously for it to look like I had money saved up and available. There are formulas the Mexican Immigration uses to calculate eligibility. Some of the links and resources I used personally are listed on the resource page at the end of this book.

If I couldn't qualify for a temporal visa, I would be forced to just get a tourist visa and make border runs every 180 days to receive another six-month visa. The Lakeside area where I was moving is an eleven-hour drive to the Laredo, TX border. Also, from the information I was gathering via online and the Facebook groups the Mexican government had started cracking down and it wasn't a guarantee that the tourist visa would automatically be renewed for another 180 days. In some instances, people were being given just 90-day visas. I didn't want to be caught up in that mess.

But first things first. I needed to gather the required documents to apply for the temporal Mexican visa. Most states have a consulate office where you would apply. However, there are states that do not have a consulate office and people have been known to drive over to another state to apply. You will need to research if your state has one or not. Luckily Atlanta has a Mexican Consulate Office. I would need to bring:

✓ the actual application (which I downloaded and printed off from the Ministry of Foreign Affairs website listed in resources)
✓ original and copies of financial statements
✓ original and copies of passport

✓ one frontal picture (passport size, minimum: 3.2cm x 2.6)

✓ payment. (The fee is $24 dollars at this time)

That seemed simple enough to me, until I begin attempting to fill out the application on line. I had been studying and practicing Spanish, but not enough to navigate the site and application. I downloaded Google Translate on my phone and kept it near. What a process that was! But I wasn't working any longer and could devote the time, effort and dedication it took to not throw my hands up and hire a lawyer to handle it. I took it on as a challenge, it became fun and consumed my days. I filled out, downloaded and printed out the application. I obtained copies of my financial statements and went to CVS and had passport pictures taken. I read somewhere that you had to go on line and make an appointment to have an interview. I had no such luck, so I called the number provided on the website. When I finally got someone, I was told just to show up during business hours. I've always said that the stars aligned for me to move abroad. I felt very strongly that moving abroad was indeed part of my life's journey. As I write this, I noticed the date I received my residency. It was 7/11/2017. I dabble a bit in numerology and I can honestly state those numbers are significant in their own right. That date fell on a Tuesday, which is my day of birth, also extremely significant. All that is to say, on the day I went to the consulate office, the stars aligned. I went with my fingers crossed, praying and hoping I qualified for a Temporal Visa, that day… and I received a Residente Permanente Visa!

I arrived at the consulate in Atlanta around 9:00am. I was directed to sit in an area and wait to be called. After sitting in that area for about 20 minutes without being given a number or anything I stepped up to a man in uniform. I told him I was there to get a visa. I was thinking, "How are they going call me without giving me a number or having me sign in?" He told me to follow him. He led me upstairs to another area where he directed me to sit and wait. There was one other gentleman already sitting in this small area. Eventually, two more people came to sit and wait. All I knew is that I was second in line.

After waiting another 30 minutes a young gentleman stepped out his office and spoke to the first gentleman, asking questions in Spanish. The guy was fluent in Spanish and answered the questions. The gentleman then walked over to me and asked me if I was retired. I told him yes. He took all of my documents and said, "Okay" then ducked back into his office. He returned about 20 minutes later with the first guy's documents and a handshake. He then turned to me and said he needed me to email him my credit union statements because something that was supposed to show was not showing. He gave me his email address and I sat there and quickly complied. He ducked back into his office. Maybe another 20 or so minutes passed, and he called my name to step into his office. It appeared all was well, he had received the email and had documents stapled and stamped. He gave me a slip to pay the cashier downstairs and told me it would be a few hours before the visa would be ready for pick up. I thanked him, shook his hand and hurried to go pay. When the cashier said $36 dollars, it didn't click, I thought, oh they must have gone up in price and haven't posted it on the website yet.

I really don't remember how I spent the next few hours before I returned to pick up my visa. I went directly back upstairs after a few hours and took my same seat. The interviewer was speaking to one of the people who had come in after me. He finished up that conversation, went in his office and came back out with my passport and Mexican visa stamped inside. I was so excited, I just grabbed it, thanked him and left! It wasn't until I got in my car and took a thorough look at the visa stamped in my passport, that I discovered it said Residente Permanente! I flashed back to the office scene when this young gentleman stated that the regular person was on vacation and that he was filling in. That wonderful, beautiful and probably not as experienced as he should have been young man gave me my residency and it was permanent!

I equate the scene to shooting craps, which I did quite a bit when I lived in Las Vegas. For those of you who know the game, it felt like I rolled the dice on the Mexican Immigration craps table and was praying for a point...temporal, instead I threw a 7 or it could have been an 11. Doesn't really matter. What does matter is that I came out a winner on 7/11/2017.

I had completed the first part of the visa process. The second part would take place south of the border, where I would receive my green card. That in and of itself is a process. There was much more research on my part to do to learn the actual steps needed to complete the process. Once in Mexico, I had 30 days from the day I entered the country to begin the process of finalizing my residency. I arrived in Mexico on Friday, December 1, 2017.

On Monday, December 4th I found my way to the National Migration Institute Office (INM) located in Chapala. Basically, on that visit I was just registering (within the confines of the 30 days) that I was present in the country and available to complete the process. Once I registered, I could not leave the country until the process was complete. There are exceptions to that rule, however it requires a written notarized letter, which I'm assuming could be an added headache. I was keeping positive thoughts that no major incident took place in the states that would need my immediate attention until the process was over. Once registered, I could return for the next step when I had all the required documents. No appointment was needed.

As I left the office that day, I realized there were two items from the required list that I could take care of that day, which were the visa photos and the receipt from a bank showing I paid for the visa. No money is ever collected at the INM office. I headed out of the office with the directions the nice lady at the counter gave me as to where the bank was located, it was pretty easy, I actually walked to Santander Bank, a block before the main road in Chapala.

After completing the transaction, I asked the teller where I could get a photo taken. I left the bank with the directions given from the teller. I walked up the street to the corner of the main road and turned right. I was feeling confident about the progress I was making. It turned out that the barber shop/photo copy place was not where they took photos for visas but made photo copies. I guess my request got lost in translation with the teller. The barber, whose English was as limited as my Spanish, and I fumbled through hand gestures and our limited vocabulary until I understood where I needed to go. It was across the main road and maybe a block and a half past the plaza on the same side of the street. I couldn't miss it, and I didn't.

It was a very small studio painted green on the outside. There were no other customers when I arrived. I told the lady behind the counter that I needed a visa photograph. She took me right in. I was instructed to remove all jewelry and not to smile. After getting my photo taken, which I hated because it was so unflattering with no smiling, I was informed by the photographer it would be 20 to 30 minutes before it would be ready. I took advantage of this time to walk around Chapala's plaza and market area. I bought a freshly blended green juice and sat on a bench in the plaza feeling quite proud of myself having arrived only four days earlier.

I went back to the INM office a week and a half later. I remember wanting to get all my documents in before they closed for the holiday. It was rumored that they would be closed until mid-January. This time when I arrived at the office I had in my possession;

- Original and copies of passport
- FMM form that was stamped at the airport with date of entry
- Original and copies of Mexican visa
- Online application which is different from the online application I gave the consulate in Atlanta. It's called Formato Basico
- Three visa sized photos
- Receipts showing I paid $4,500 pesos (approximately $250US)

I arrived early morning and was fifth in line to sign in once the doors opened. When my name was called, I proudly stepped up to the desk and handed over all documents. It appeared all was going well until the counter clerk noticed a discrepancy on my Formato Basico online application. My middle name, was not on the application and it must match perfectly with my American passport and Mexican visa. I was devastated! I was so close. The counter clerk called over her supervisor who explained I would have to redo the application, print it out and bring it back as she handed me back all my documents. Where could I do that? I asked. She stated that there was a computer place and pointed up toward the main road in Chapala where I could redo the application and print it out. "What time do you close? I asked. She stated 1 p.m. It was 9:45 a.m, no worries. I got this, or so I thought.

Leaving the office, I decided to walk up to the main road like I did before when I went to the bank to pay. I assumed as soon as I got to the main road I would ask around and promptly be pointed in the right direction of the computer place. I just chuckled to myself as I typed this and reminisced on my mindset during that time. I made it to the main road and went back to the barber/photo copy place since he had been so helpful before and asked about a computer place, so I could print something out. It appeared he understood exactly what I was saying, he nodded his head and said, "Si." I would later come to learn most Mexicans do not like to say "no" or "I don't know" when asked questions. Bless his heart, he pointed me in a direction and off I went crossing the main road and heading down some blocks looking for any sign or indication of computers for public use.

After walking a few blocks and not seeing anything, I popped my head into a welcoming office. The outside sign said "Abogado de Inmigracion." A nice lady walked up to me and I begin telling her my story until she said, "No habla Ingles." A gentleman walked up at that moment and asked if he could help me. He spoke perfect English, I thought cool! Surely this man will do me this one solid and allow me to print this one freaking document off as courtesy, right? He took me in his office, pulled up the site where the document was and begin asking questions to fill in the blanks. I began answering the questions and then just handed him same document to copy explaining I had everything I needed I just needed to put my middle name on the document and how I appreciate him doing this for me. He stated he would do it for 500 pesos! I quickly snatched the document back and stated I didn't have any money. I told him never mind and walked out.

I took a deep breath, looked around, and realized I was lost deep within a Chapala neighborhood. I started walking left, and somehow wound up back on the main road by a 7-Eleven and a bull ring. I went into the store and asked, "Habla Ingles?" The response was "No "and a head shake. I left and started walking back towards the corner where the main road and carretera meet. There were stores of all sorts on both sides of the street, and lots of people walking to and fro. I stopped in a cell store and questioned, "Habla Ingles?" Again, I was met with a head shake and "No. "

This experience was leading me to recall my research on Chapala that said Chapala is mainly a Mexican and Spanish speaking town. I remembered thinking that if I was to live there I would have really have to be on point with my Spanish or immediately submerse myself in classes.

As I continued to walk up the street, I checked my cell phone for the time. It was 11:11am. I quicken my pace and swayed my head from one side of the street to the other looking for a sign of some sort that I could recognize. Lo and behold the word "Internet" was on a sign across the street. I made my way across and entered the open space. I saw computers! There were maybe six all together, and it was obvious that this was a business where people could come in and utilize the computers for a fee. A young lady was helping a customer at the desk, so I pointed to the computers and she motioned for me to go ahead. I brought up the website and begin filling out the form. Midway through the application it asked for an email address, for the life of me I couldn't find the "@" symbol on the Spanish keyboard. The attendant was still busy with customers and I was running out of time. I held my hand up and waved it vigorously, my impatience showing. Thinking back on it all now, I'm sure my gestures were considered rude. Finally, she came over and I pointed to my half-typed email address. She hit two keys simultaneously and voila the "@" sign appeared. I completed the application, printed it out and paid. To this day, I not sure what keys she hit, or how much it cost. It must not have been much though.

I dashed out and continued walking up the street tired and thirsty. I was going to catch the bus back to the office, but one never appeared, and I walked all the way back to the INM office. I arrived back around 12:30 pm, I signed in again and took a seat. In just a few minutes I was called to the counter by the supervisor who recognized me from earlier that morning. She took my paperwork, looked it over stamped a few items and printed out a document. She handed me the document as if to say, "Here you go. I'm sure you know what to do next." I did. The document provided had a NUT number (it's like a social security number), a Pieza number, a password and the website. I was to continue to check the website until I received the "approved" message, which meant I could return to the INM office give them my visa pictures and be finger printed. This could take up to two weeks or longer. I checked the website every day.

When I received the approval message, I went back to the office and was finger printed.  On January 17, 2018 I went and picked up my Residente Permanente card. I think it's funny that my residency card is actually green. From the start of my visa journey stateside on 7/11/2017 to 1/17/2018 it took a total of six months. I did it myself.

**Consider the visa requirements and process when planning and preparing to live abroad.** Consider exactly what type of visa will work best for your situation. Also, consider hiring a lawyer to complete the visa process. If you do it yourself, it takes patience and strict attention to detail. Organization of required documents is essential as well. The visa process starts in the country where you currently reside and is completed in the country to which you are moving. Every country has their own process and requirements and you must thoroughly research the criteria needed. It can be time consuming and intimidating, especially if there is a language barrier. Ever spent a day in the DMV office trying to change a title, address or renew your license? Finally, you're called up only to be told you don't have the correct whatever. Obtaining a visa can be like that scene on steroids. Especially if you are doing it alone. Not that it can't be done; it most definitely can. My experience is proof of that.

I posted this on FaceBook the day I received my Residente Permanante Visa. I was at my favorite watering hole in my town. On that day the margarita tasted oh so sweet—like victory.

# Chapter Four

# Consider: Research

Research is my thing. It's a strong part of my skill set that developed over time during my career in education. I recall listening to a professional football player being interviewed years ago. He was asked what he loved most about playing the game. He stated, "Everything! I love the smell of the turf, the sound of helmets colliding with each other, the taste of victory after winning a game, the feel of the football in my hand, and watching the fans cheer." I am not a football fan, however I understood exactly what the player was expressing in that interview.

When I began my teaching career, I loved everything about it. The smell of ink from the ditto machine in the teachers' workroom, the sound of kids playing on the playground, the feel of the pointer in my hand as I taught from the board, watching my students grow through the year, and creating meaningful lessons to engage them. Research is a big part of teaching. I was always on the hunt to find and deliver lessons that would open my student's eyes to the joy of learning. I was planning on living in another country, and research of that country was essential. Of course, we've come a long way since ditto machines. The world, and anything I wanted to know about it, was just a click away. Another skill that I have, which I also attribute to my career in education, is organization. When I'm acquiring tons of information, I have a knack for organizing it in a way that I can put my finger back on a document when needed. In this chapter I'll discuss some essentials that should be researched thoroughly, where I found the information, and how I organized it.

I belong to certain Facebook groups specific to the area where I chose to live. I'm always amazed at the blanket questions people ask concerning important issues like housing, banking, visas, and healthcare. They ask questions like, "What's the best way to go about getting healthcare?" It's like they want all the research someone else did to be given to them on a silver platter, and that's not how any of that is supposed to work. Facebook groups can be vicious, and I've witnessed people being cyber-attacked for having audacity to ask such blanket questions. I'm not saying questions shouldn't and can't be asked. Lord knows I had my share of questions. However, there is a Facebook group etiquette and it's better to ask questions, as part of your research. For instance, I remember asking a question about bringing my car across the border. At that time, I was planning on taking my car. I remember asking, "I have a 2007 Chevy Colbalt, and I plan on packing it to the rim, and attaching a small trailer. Once I cross, is it possible to sell the trailer as I won't need it anymore?" Generous answers poured in about crossing the border (discussed in Chapter 7), that I added to my own research.

Research takes time, organization, and dedication. I was dedicated to uncovering as much information as I could as it related to my way of living as comfortably as possible. It is my life and I couldn't leave it in the hands of anyone else. I had to discover and know for myself. By the time I was finished researching the when, where, how, and what (I already knew the why) of Lakeside I was extremely knowledgeable about the ins and outs of everyday living. Whenever I took a break from researching, I was on Google Street View going up and down the carretera (main road) and throughout the neighborhoods. My dedication to exploring and getting to know my area was so intense that I felt like I was actually there, going to the open markets, walking to Walmart, catching the bus into Ajijic, Chapala, and certain restaurants I wanted to try once I arrived. I wanted to know how to get around on the bus without having to ask anyone. I wanted to be completely self-sufficient. Four months prior to departing I spent the better part of my day daydreaming, focusing my attention and setting intentions. I had an entire schedule of what I was going to do every day for the first five days after my arrival.

After deciding on the specific region of Mexico where I wanted to move, I started researching the towns and rentals. One thing I was already sure of is that I was going to rent. I was not interested in buying. The channels I used for my research were Google, YouTube, and Facebook groups specific to the content I was researching. As I looked for a rental, I started with my Facebook groups. I joined groups like Lake Chapala Rentals, Lake Chapala Rentals by Owner, and Access Lake Chapala. There were also websites like Century 21 and Lake Chapala Realty that I visited periodically. What's good about being in groups on Facebook is that you are alerted whenever there is a new posting. I checked those sites and groups almost every day, taking notes. In doing this, I became very clear on what I wanted and what I could and wouldn't accept. For instance, being centrally located was very important because I wouldn't have a car. Some people are very particular about furnishings and wouldn't dare dream of renting a place that's already furnished. I didn't have a problem with a furnish place, but it did have to have a certain style and feel that appealed to me. Also, I needed the rent to fit my small monthly budget. Fortunately I found my place on Chapala Rentals. I rent from a private owner who was nice enough to do a walk-through video for me and allowed for a security deposit to hold it for six weeks in advance until I arrived. My landlord was waiting for me at my condo the day I arrived to collect the first month's rent and hand over the keys.

When researching visa requirements I used Google. I simply put in "How do I obtain a Mexican visa?" Of course I was led to multiple sites to begin researching; some were helpful and others not so much. When I researched what living in the Lakeside area was like I went to YouTube and simply put in, "Lake Chapala Mexico" and up popped Jerry Brown Travels. I immediately subscribed. I was happy anytime I got a notice that a new video from Jerry had posted. Surprisingly enough, I now occasionally hike with Jerry and his lovely wife Lori. If you were to type in "Lake Chapala Mexico" my video in which Jerry interviewed me pops up, which I think is super cool. There are many couples and single people all over the world vlogging, videotaping experiences instead of writing about them (blogging), and relaying information in real time. I followed Jerry's channel pretty exclusively because that's where I was moving. However, I watched several videos from a couple in Costa Rica, another in Columbia and a young lady in Thailand. Videos really gave me a sense of a truer experience.

After learning I was moving to Mexico, friends would ask, "What are you going to do all day, every day in Mexico? It was a good question and it fueled my research to a certain degree because... what was I going to do? It led me to start visually creating a lifestyle and life that I wanted for myself when I arrived. I've lived alone ever since my daughter went off to college in 2012. I enjoy entertaining myself, and I'm actually pretty good at it. In the states when I was home alone I would color, journal, watch TV, play music, read, play games on my tablet, talk on the phone and engage in social media. I still saw myself doing those things in Mexico. But I did begin questioning myself, wondering about what activities I wanted to be involved in when I wasn't relaxing at home. Lakeside has such an active expat community it was truly a smorgasbord of activities to consider. I don't remember exactly what I typed in or ran across on Facebook that led me to the Ajijic Hiking Group. I was intrigued, joined the group and started following it. The pictures posted of the different hikes were beautiful. I've always loved nature even though my entire life has been spent in big urban cities; Detroit, Las Vegas, and Atlanta.

Hiking appealed to me and I wanted to try it. Boy, was it a rough start! I was overweight, inexperienced and not use to the altitude. The easiest hike offered is to what is called the Chapel. Lakeside is 5,000 ft. above sea level, and the hike to the Chapel is 500 ft of zigzag incline. It's for beginners lead by a really nice hike leader named Gary. I began hiking to the Chapel with Gary and Maddy (his friend's dog) twice a week. I was amazed at the hikers 10 and 15 years my senior laughing, chatting, breathing easy and not sweating profusely. I, on the other hand, was a hot mess! Totally intimidated yet motivated at the same time. I even fell several times throughout that first month, but luckily didn't break anything. Gary was patient and encouraging, as were the other hikers. I have met some of the most fascinating people from all over the world on my hikes. Some hikers have become really good friends and are part of my tribe here. I fell in love with hiking; well let's just say it's a love/hate relationship. I hate it going up, it's so challenging, but when I reach the top I'm so damn proud of myself, and that it never gets old. I don't do Gary's hike anymore, I've move on to more challenging hikes, but he picks me up every hike day.

Yoga was another interest I had but never pursued stateside. It looked like something I could get into and possibly enjoy. I imagined it to be candles, incense, soft music, a mat, and good stretching out of my body. There is a yoga studio a couple blocks from where I live. I had just started thinking about possibly practicing yoga when a hiker made that very suggestion. He said lots of hikers practiced yoga because it helps enhance balance and coordination. "Stretching your muscles out a few times a week keeps you limber," he stated. It wasn't long after that conversation that I tried my first yoga class. There were no candles or incense burning in the studio, but it had a really nice feel to it. Soft music does play throughout the hour-long practice and I'm provided with a mat, blocks, and belts with which to practice. Again, I encountered people, mostly women, who were 10 and 15 years my senior moving in and out of poses with ease and grace. I, however, struggled with getting up and down off the floor. By the time I managed to move myself into what could be consider a semblance of the pose called for, the group had moved on to the next pose. Again, I let the intimidation of it all be my motivation. Those women inspired me. I wanted to be a better version of myself physically and began combining hiking with yoga. I now hike twice a week, and I practice yoga three times a week. Thus, five days a week I'm doing something physical.

I'm an animal lover. I grew up with a loving German Shepherd (Missy) and raised my kids with 2 beautiful dogs

(Mikey & Sweetpea). Through research I learned about the street dog population in my area. There are many strays that roam the streets in and around the towns. They are the most chilled animals you'd ever want to see. Most have lived on the streets all their lives. They don't bother me, and I have yet to have one follow me. There are a several dog and cat rescues and many very involved expats who volunteer at those rescues. I made a mental note that volunteering at an animal shelter was something I was going to definitely look into. Some of my hiker friends participate with the rescues and have welcomed me to tag along with them whenever I have some extra time. I certainly will when my plate clears a little.  I also want to do some volunteering at the local community theater. I like working backstage, prop making/painting, sound, lights and staging.

A lot of my research was driven by how I saw myself living in Mexico. I tried not to leave any stone unturned as it related to my way of being, so that when I left my home country I would be as comfortable as possible in my new country.  I was learning about Mexico and the area in which I chose to live. I created a binder with tabs for the notes I was taking and I created file folders for things I was printing out that had to do with visas and rentals. Oh, I was organized to a fault!

As I planned and prepared, searching for a rental proved to be ongoing throughout the year. There wasn't much I could do as far as putting a deposit down because I was too far out from my arrival date. But I still looked at rentals often, and doing so gave me a better idea of the towns and villages Lakeside and what they uniquely had to offer for my individual taste and lifestyle. My research included viewing pictures and videos, reading reviews, reading blogs, asking questions on Facebook groups, reading articles, and talking to people who had experienced the particular topic being researched at the time. One click led to another, then another, and yet another until all leads had been run down and information exhausted on the particulaR topic. Along with visas, rentals, monthly expenses, healthcare, and transportation, I also researched:

✓ the best way for me to continue to watch my television shows
✓ where I could get documents printed
✓ where I could get a manicure and pedicure
✓ how was I to handle mail
✓ what were the crime rates
✓ where the clinics and hospitals were located and their hours operation
✓ where and how to go about catching a bus, taxi or Uber
✓ how is the Internet connections in the area
✓ restaurants I wanted to try
✓ local doctor and dentist reviews
✓ how was the local entertainment scene

Fifty percent of my research was conducted while following Facebook threads in the groups that were specific to the area where I was moving. I belonged to several groups where I checked and followed threads daily. When questions were asked that were pertinent to what I was researching I took notes and followed leads given in the answers. Most times answers led to more questions and more research outside the group. I researched until I was comfortable with my own knowledge and information on a topic. I had become a regular in the groups and occasionally, I participated in the topic of discussion because I had done my research and could contribute valuable information. I began meeting and making friends in those groups who were by then anticipating my arrival and they continued to offer help, encouragement and advice outside of the group.

One such friend was instrumental in helping to make my move even possible. If it were not for her, I probably wouldn't have made my planned arrival date of December 1, 2017. It was in the late afternoon of November 30, 2017 that my plans for how I was going to depart the next morning blew up in my face. I had my three boxes and three storage bins packed tightly and wrapped in moving plastic situated in the garage, waiting to be loaded into a friend's truck for a 5:00 am ride to the airport the next morning. My two suitcases were still in my room waiting to be brought down and loaded as well. With time on my hand and anticipation in my heart, I posted on my Facebook page something like, "In less than 24 hours I and my eight pieces of luggage will be landing in Mexico. I'm so excited I probably won't sleep a wink!" Not too long after that post I received a private message from one of my now friends I met in one of the groups. She messaged me, "Hey Queen, I use to work for Delta airlines and I know that during certain times of the year they invoke an embargo on how much luggage you can bring into the country. I don't know if they still do but you might want to check it out just to be safe." She also left the link for me to check it out. I remember thinking to myself in that moment as I clicked on the link, yeah, they probably don't do that anymore. No sooner had that thought came and went from me, I was staring at the dates for Delta's luggage embargo. Indeed, there was an embargo and it started on December 1, 2017 and ended on January 15, 2018. In that instant my throat dropped into my stomach and I stared in disbelief at the computer screen. I don't remember how long it took for me to gather myself, but when I did, I started making phone calls. So many calls were made to the airline, so many holds, so many departments, and finally other calls to other airlines to no avail. With each call I became more desperate and more freaked out. How could this be happening on the eve of my departure!

I often talk about how the stars aligned for me during and after my move to Mexico. This is another situation, along with my permanent visa, that proves my theory. My neighbors in the states are Mexican, a large family that adopted me not long after I moved next door to them. For four years they have looked out for me, shared meals, laughs, family celebrations and from time to time money when things were tight. I tutored the young ones and helped the adults with paperwork when English was a barrier. They were my extended family. I remember the day I told them I was moving to Mexico and why. They were so surprised and happy for me I guess they knew it was a great decision. But it was when I told them *where* in Mexico and they celebrated with such enthusiasm I had to ask, "Y'all know the area?" Not only did they know the area, they were *from* the area! They are from the south side of the lake. Literally, across the lake from me! Boy did we celebrate that day. In all the years I had known them I had never thought to ask what part of Mexico they were from. Every year the family loads up their Escalade, attaches their trailer to it, full of pretty much anything you can think of to take back to Mexico, and they stay for months. I'd been invited to go with them three out of the four years I've lived next door. They always brought something back for me each time; a bottle of tequila, a rosary that was blessed, and a sombrero.

On that evening before I was to leave, after discovering my luggage could and would not be accompanying me, I was completely distraught and in tears as I went over to say my goodbyes. As I told them my dilemma and how I didn't see myself moving to another country without my things, the matriarch of the family was making a phone call. Watch the stars align. Come to find out my Mexican family had a relative with a van and trailer who (just so happen) was going to be traveling to the Lakeside area on December 8th, arriving around December 11th. After Mama got off the phone with him, he was on his way over to see if he could fit my three boxes and three storage bins aLong with the other things he was taking. An hour later we were all standing in my garage discussing price, which was completely reasonable given the circumstances, and the fact I was going to pay a few hundred more above his price had the luggage flown with me. Right then and there he loaded up my boxes and bins, received payment and disappeared into the night. I breathed a sigh of relief, thanked my Mexican family and made a mental note to seek out my Facebook friend to personally thank her and take her out to lunch. Who knows? Had I not been active in the Facebook group, had I not made that post, had my Facebook friend not informed me of the luggage embargo, I would have been dropped off at the Atlanta airport with my eight pieces of luggage at 5:30 am only to be told at the ticket counter that I could only take two pieces of luggage! That would have caused a mental breakdown for me, of that I am sure.

I arrived at the airport that next morning with two pieces of luggage which contained my clothes and toiletries. I figured I could make it with just that until my personal things arrived, because my condo was fully furnished.

**Consider extensive research when planning and preparing to live abroad.** It is extremely important that your interests are accessible and represented in the local area where you decide to move. Will that area fit the lifestyle and way of being you are envisioning for yourself? If you're moving alone, as I did, will you feel safe? It's personal because you are attempting to create a way of being comfortable in a foreign land. I researched and researched and researched what I felt were all aspects of my way of being and living comfortably but still missed a very important component, a luggage embargo. Goes to show that you may not think of or catch every aspect but get as close as you can. Be as thorough as possible in your research, and may the stars align even if you miss a component.

## Chapter Five

# Consider: Downsizing

I lived 20 minutes south of the Hartsfield-Jackson Atlanta International Airport, in a 3 bedroom, 2 1/2 bath home with an attached garage in Clayton County, Georgia. Aside from the master which contained a full bath, each bedroom was large enough with a front and back portion to be separate. The house was surrounded by trees at the end of a cul-de-sac, with a huge front yard and even larger fenced in backyard. The long front porch had two rocking chairs and a small table between them, garnished with citronella candles. Every room had become completely furnished over the four years that I lived there. It was a big house with built in shelving units that ran along a brick fireplace in the great room, which also included a pool table. The dining room contained a 5-piece dining set, as did the kitchen. The living room had adequate walking around space even though it contained two sofas, large chair, cocktail table, end tables, and a 52-inch screen television and stand. There was artwork, mirrors, pictures, and wall decor, in every room throughout the entire house. In four short years many memories were made there. It served well for birthday parties, fish fries, holiday festivities, barbecues, an Airbnb, a family reunion, a haven for family members to rest and get it figured out, and porch time. My friends have visited from across the country, sat in the rocking chairs and enjoyed the energy from that southern front porch.

So how does one take 50 plus years of accumulated "things" and decide what stays and what goes when moving abroad? Before I had even secured my 1 bedroom 1 bath condo in Mexico I knew that wherever I landed in Mexico, the place would be furnished. Therefore, I needed to downsize my "things" drastically. Truth is, I was at a point in my life where I could, with the least amount of resistance, let go of the furniture, the dishes, the decor, the books, the tapes, the holiday decorations, knick-knacks, the career leftovers, the files, and 90% of the clothes I wasn't wearing. The thought was immensely liberating.

Once the decision was made to move abroad, and planning and preparing had begun, I started thinking in terms of categories. Being organized is a big part of my personality. So, in terms of downsizing, there were six big questions needing answers: What was I keeping, buying, donating, selling, giving away or throwing away? The keeping category was easy. There are "things" that represent the very core or essence of a person. Those "things" are personal, and no explanation is needed. They stay close to a person. More often than not, those "things" could be found in a person's bedroom. At least that's the case for me; my bedroom is my haven. So most "things" associated with my bedroom were automatically in the keeping category.

As I followed the Facebook group threads I got an idea of what needed to be bought and brought along with me. I learned most things could be purchased in my area or in Guadalajara, which was a 30-minute drive from my town. I was amused at discovering how media had shaped my image about life in Mexico. It is not a third world country and every amenity afforded me in the states is afforded south of the border. There is a Walmart within a 10-minute walk from where I live. There is a store in my town that caters specifically to North American taste, at a higher price of course.

However, there were some "things" where a line was drawn in the sand and I purchased north of the border and brought with me those things necessary for my personal comfort:

- ✓ Towels
- ✓ Pillows
- ✓ Linen and foam mattress pad
- ✓ Bras/panties
- ✓ Kitchenware
- ✓ Set of knives
- ✓ Hair and skin care products

Donating was an ongoing process throughout the year and whatever I didn't sell was eventually donated along with the things already marked for donation. A new thrift store and donation center had recently opened in a shopping plaza near my home, so dropping off had become a regular routine for me. After a while, I stopped accepting the charitable statements given after drops offs for tax purposes. There is only so much I could allot for tax purposes anyway. I also had a charitable organization who would come and pick up a load right in the driveway. I would gather a load of various household items, cover it with a sheet then first thing in the morning a truck would back into my driveway and load up. They were always mindful to leave the sheet and my tax statement. Each time I dropped off a load, or had one picked up, I felt lighter inside. It was an amazing feeling. One of my guest rooms became moving central. The front part of the room was for what was being kept or purchased, and the back part of the room was for what was being donated. Anything I was selling stayed in its original location until sold. I continued to throw away the unsellable, useless to me in Mexico, and nobody wanted items throughout the downsizing process.

I count it a blessing not to possess a spirit of hoarding, whereas one could always find reason as to how some "thing" will have an eventual value or use sometime in the future. Hoarders hold on to items waiting on an imagined use for them while adding and holding on to more and more "things". I can't watch the show "Hoarders" for that very reason; it makes me itch. My heart goes out to people suffering with hoarding issues. It is truly psychologically crippling. The hardest donation for me was my library. I had always been an avid reader and I kept most of my undergrad, and master's degree text books. I had worked on my doctorate for some years and came within 3 courses of my dissertation, but it wasn't to be, I know now that it was not my path. I had a World Book encyclopedia set I purchased for the kids when they were very young. I believe that set was utilized all of one time by my kids. They were 90's kids and were being taught to research through the information highway of the internet. I also had a hardcover collection of a 12-book series called Left Behind and many personal books on a plethora of topics. Back when I was Ubering, I met an enthusiastic young lady. She and I hit it off immediately. We struck up a conversation as she shared her life's testimony, as riders often did with me. We connected on Facebook shortly after that first day, and I've kept up with her as she has with me. I had a very large spiritual book collection and it was my great pleasure to bless her with that box of books. I gave a good portion of books to my expectant daughter for her to start her child's library. Four other boxes followed to friends and family whom I knew shared the same love of a particular genre as I did. Dispersing my books was like peeling back onion layers of myself, but at the same time it felt amazing blessing people with treasures. I kept a handful of books that are the very core of me and they came with me.

Because I had a big, fully furnished home I first thought that having an estate sell would be the way to go in the sell category. I began researching how to go about having one. The idea of having multiple garage sales was not appealing to me for two reasons. One was I lived in a cul-de-sac three left turns off the main road deep in the back of the community. Not much traffic ever went that deep in the cut unless a person lived back there. Secondly, the thought of hauling things out and setting up tables was out the question, and strangers off the street walking around my home was not going to happen either. I soon learned that successful estate sales for the most part are run by estate sale service companies. They come into your home, complete an evaluation of your things, do all the advertising, staging and tagging. They also set prices and generally take 30% of the profits. I had a really nice place. But an actual estate sale by a company was out of my league.

As I downsized, there were four avenues I used to sell my things. I used Facebook Market, Offer Up, Let Go and My Neighborhood. The latter is a private community website for residents to communicate news, sell, advertise services and announce community events. I was amazed at how easy it was to register on the sites and start posting. I enjoyed staging the items, taking pictures and then posting for sale. Wall decor and artwork moved quickly through the sites. It's something about having just what someone needed or had been looking for that makes the sale even sweeter. A very nice gentleman bought my mini refrigerator for his wife's office, my wet bar went to a lady who had kicked her husband out for the fifth and last time. My bedroom TV went to an 11-year-old who had gotten a good report card. My living room and bedroom set went to a young lady who was moving into her first apartment. The sales went on and on, and so did the stories. At times it got awfully hectic communicating with multiple buyers. I learned the language of selling online quickly and my 'things' did indeed sell. I also sold several home items to my oldest brother and now when I visit Atlanta, I get a kick out of seeing them well taken care of and looking very nice in their new home.

The living room set sold was to the daughter of a friend, who I worked with at the railyard. Her daughter was moving into her own apartment. It had been raining for a few days straight and the ground was very soft the day my friend and her daughter came to pick up the furniture. They had rented an open-bed U-Haul pickup truck and brought plastic to cover things, just in case. I marveled at her and her daughter as they removed cushions and then the sofas and big chair themselves. I didn't think twice as I told them to back the truck up through a wide patch of earth with trees arching on both sides, and up to the front porch. The truck was loaded with no problem. It started to lightly sprinkle, threatening to rain any minute. My friend got in her car, which was loaded with the cushions, and the daughter climbed behind the wheel of the truck. It didn't hit any of us that the truck was now too heavy to make it back across that open patch of earth until it was too late. The daughter started the truck and went maybe two feet before the wheels planted themselves deep into the wet, muddy patch. No problem, right? We advised her to back up, try again...back up try again, back up and try yet again. After several attempts the truck was good and stuck. We tried bricks, cardboard and plain stubbornness to try and get the truck out to no avail.

I had a long-paved driveway leading to an attached garage. Being that the earth was so soft because of the recent rains, common sense should have told me that backing the truck up to the front door and then filling it with two sofas and a big chair was a bad idea. But sometimes, common sense isn't common. All I was thinking was "It's only ten steps from my living room to the front door. It's a double door too, so plenty room." Otherwise they would have had to go through the dining room's narrow doorway, through the kitchen, down two steps through the family room and out through the narrow door to the garage. That's what I was thinking.

A neighbor hearing ongoing revving of the truck had mercy on me, and came over to help. The truck continued to dig in deeper. Another neighbor came over to assist, who called yet another neighbor over. Now armed with a group of people, one suggested to another that maybe their truck could be used to pull the "stuck deep as hell in the mud" truck out. "Anybody have tow cables?" someone asked. My neighbors to the left of me luckily had some and they were attached to the U-Haul. The rescue of the very stuck pickup ensued with cheers and high fives, as if they were rescuing a stuck animal or human. What a spectacle that turned out to be. I was so grateful to my neighbors and embarrassed at the same time. I was certain, "What the hell were you thinking?" was foremost in their minds as they smiled, waved and walked back to their respective homes. As I stood on my front porch and viewed the muddy massacre of my lawn I made a note to myself, "Don't you ever do something that dumb again!"

I was the mom who started and updated my kids' baby books religiously. I have one of each, a boy who is 28 years old at the writing of this, and a 25-year-old daughter, who is married and has a young son of her own. Both their baby books were completed around age 7. I then started scrap books for them up until they were in their late teens. Those books contained their pay check stub from their first job, their academic and athletic awards, school pictures, report cards, baptism records etc. I was "that" mom. I kept a file on both of them which contained medical records, standardized test results, social security cards, resumes and school transcripts. As I was in the throes of downsizing, I created a box for each of them. The boxes included a shared disbursement of their photographs from school, books from my library I wanted them to have, and certain mementos I knew were special to them. For example, my daughter made a refrigerator magnet in third grade which was an acronym that spelled out her name and the characteristics she believed she possessed. She was 8 years old at the time. That magnet had been on every refrigerator in every place we lived from the time she brought it home. It was to be her cherished memory now, not mine. Preparing those boxes for my kids was like making another scrapbook, and I enjoyed liberating myself from all the things that I held on to that truly belonged to them at this point in my life. I had to mail my daughter her boxes, as she lives in the state of Oregon. My son lives in Atlanta, and he was able to stop by on one of his visits and pick his boxes up. A year later as I visited both their homes on my first state side visit after moving to Mexico, I took note that both had stuffed the boxes under a piece of furniture in their homes. I quietly smiled to myself. I felt lighter having released their "things" to them.

Another aspect of downsizing for me was ridding myself of paper. I had two file cabinets full of files, and seven shoeboxes full of paper! One file cabinet was personal; it contained files on any and everything pertaining to my life, and my family. Also, files that I kept from various workshops and conferences I had attended throughout my career. Another file cabinet was mainly for work. A teacher's work seldom stops once the end of the day bell rings. Once I got home the second part of the job began; completing lesson plans, checking papers, and phone conferences with parents was a nightly routine. I've always said that the teaching profession sadly is a very trendy profession. Every year it seemed to me that the higher ups came up with a new and improved way to teach children. Unfortunately, teachers had very little input on the curriculum being shoved down their throats to teach. There was the new math era, the whole language era, the No Child Left Behind era, and now the Common Core curriculum, each claiming to be the end all be all to improving education. Not to mention the different reading, math, and science programs that districts buy, it seems every other year, which teachers must learn and regurgitate to their students. Needless to say, I had accumulated an extreme number of files as an elementary and middle school teacher.

Part of my organization compulsion was holding on to most of my receipts throughout a given year. I kept the receipts in an envelope in my night stand. On the envelope I would write the year and January-June, because by June the envelope would be so full I would usually have to put a rubber band around it. I would then place another envelope with the year and July-December written on it and place the receipts throughout those months in there. At the end of the year, I would put those envelopes along with any other important paperwork relating to, or which would be pertinent to taxes in a shoe box. I would write the year on the shoe box and tuck it away in my closet. I was downsizing now, and I looked up on the top rack of my closet and saw seven shoeboxes (2010 -2016). I had 2003-2009 in file folders in my personal file cabinet. I didn't have a shredder, and the amount of paper I had between my file cabinets and shoeboxes would possibly blow out the motor of an average shredder if I was to purchase one. I had a medium sized fire pit in my backyard that I used on occasion when I threw a fall party. I used that fire pit to rid myself of all unnecessary paper. It was certainly a task, going through those files but the truth of the matter was I didn't need 99% of those files anymore. I was retired, moving to Mexico and starting a new life there. I burned every other day or so for about a month and then sold my file cabinets. I have a file crate here in Mexico and it has sixteen file folders. I don't see it growing any larger than that.

**Consider downsizing when planning and preparing to live abroad.** If you're like me you've lived a full life with an abundance of "things" to prove it. Downsizing can be daunting yet liberating at the same time. I can't tell you how much lighter I felt each time I rid myself of the "things" that no longer served me. "Does this serve me in any way?" is the question you must continue to ask as you begin to downsize. Everyone's situation and circumstances are different. Some people utilize moving companies and bring most of their households with them and that is a viable option. I can't speak to that because that was not my experience. I downsized 90% of my household, including my car and moved abroad. Wherever you wind up on that spectrum, consider what serves you and hold on to that. If it doesn't serve you, liberate yourself from it and move about more freely.

My three bins and three boxes delivered by my neighbor's family member on December 11, 2017.

# Chapter Six

# Consider: Healthcare

I don't have health insurance, and I am too young for Medicare. Medicare is not useable in Mexico anyway. I stopped being covered by insurance one and a half years after retiring. I couldn't afford the simplest of plans offered in the states. I now have a credit card that serves as my health insurance card. It is put away, and will only be used for health, dental and vision expenses if and when needed. Although I believe myself to be fairly healthy, I was diagnosed with rheumatoid arthritis several years ago. I very seldom have what I'd consider a flare up, but when it happens, over the counter medicine helps a great deal. I am prone to upper respiratory infections also. Once, when I was too late getting ahead my symptoms I endured a brief hospital stay. However, I usually recognize the signs when one is approaching and with a regiment of prednisone, I've been fortunate to turn things around.

I actually had one such incident the spring of my first year here in Mexico. Around Easter the entire Lakeside area blooms with purple jacaranda. Purple happens to be my favorite color and I couldn't help thinking the whole town was turning purple just for me. It was one of the most beautiful sights I had ever seen. But while feeling all warm and fuzzy with the "just for me" thoughts, my allergies were threatening a full blown respiratory attack. It never dawned on me that I was allergic to the very trees that were filling my heart with joy. I don't remember how I came to put two and two together, but once I realized it was the jacaranda trees, I knew a regiment of prednisone was needed. I walked across the street to the farmácia and asked the pharmacist in English if she had prednisone. I was shown a box of 20 tablets/50mg, and it cost $102 pesos which equals around $5.00 US. Now there are, of course a list of chronic ailments that run in my family, but I keep a close eye out and test for them with my yearly exams. I do not take any medication regularly. If I get a cold, headache, or stomach ache I try practical home remedies before purchasing an over the counter medicine. Since moving to Mexico I am much more active through hiking, yoga, and walking and I've become more in tune with my body, and its needs. This is how I live. As always everyone's health situations and circumstances are uniquely different.

In this chapter, I can only speak to what I've researched, experienced, and observed through conversations with other expats. Healthcare insurance has become extremely expensive and confusing over the years. In 2017, I was penalized for not having the insurance that I couldn't afford when I filed my taxes. The system is completely broken, and there is no quick fix. My heart bleeds for the poor and elderly. The stories of people dying because they couldn't afford their medicine are true and more common place than not. What was my strategy? I moved to Mexico.

On February 9, 2018 Fox Business published an article "The Five Countries With the Best Healthcare in the World for Retirees." Mexico was among the top five, along with Colombia, Costa Rica, Malaysia, and Panama. The article states that most doctors and dentists in Mexico received at least part of their training in the U.S., so they are familiar with the care expats expect and they speak English. Through my research I discovered that I have access to two affordable healthcare systems here: private and public. Mexico operates a public healthcare system known as Instituto Mexicano de Seguro Social (IMSS) which provides universal healthcare to Mexican families and foreign residents enrolled in the system. Expats with residency status, can purchase the insurance for a modest yearly fee, depending on age. Of course, with public healthcare there is the question of speed and quality of care. With IMSS there are waiting periods for non-emergency procedures. Members who get their coverage as part of their formal employment are given priority over those who enroll independently, as would be the case for me. The quality of care seems to vary. I've talked to expats with IMSS who say they've received good care and others who were disappointed. It's fair to say, as with all large, publicly-funded healthcare systems world-wide, that the demand for services usually exceeds the supply of resources available and compromises are always made. I found out that if I am a patient in a public hospital here I would have to depend on friends to provide bedside support and bring me food, water and toiletries when I'm admitted. They are called cuidadores (caregivers) and there are no nurses' aides or caregivers in public hospitals. When I found this out, I started trying to figure out who my team of cuidadores would be if I ever decided to sign up for IMSS. I would need at least five or six people to volunteer and work in 4-hour shifts. I imagine a husband and wife would need such a team as well. A cuidadore basically sits bedside, and no one could do that around the clock without needing a break themselves. I proposed to several people I considered close friends, that if they would be my cuidadore if or when the need arose, I would be theirs. It's a serious commitment to be someone's cuidadore. I began to imagine myself in such a scenario. I considered how important it would be for someone on my cuidadore team to have the rest of the team's contact information so that shifts could be arranged in case of an emergency. My mind is wired that way, and I became overwhelmed thinking about the organization of it all.

Another aspect about public health insurance in Mexico is blood donations. It is common for public hospitals in Mexico to require surgery candidates to find two or three blood donors. A person could wait months to have needed surgery because of the blood donation requirements. Blood donors could have a different type of blood, than the person for whom they are donating. They just have to provide the same quantity as they would need for surgery. Also, the time frame is very short from donation to the actual surgery. If a donor is rejected, which can easily happen because restrictions in Mexico for donors are some of the toughest in the world, the process for finding donations starts all over again. Requirements to donate blood include, but are not limited to, weight, age, date since last donation, no cavities, no more than three pregnancies, fasting, no alcohol or medications in the last 48 hours, and to have slept six consecutive hours. Only a small number of donors are screened each day. The lines are extremely long, so getting there early to stand in line is a must. If you're lucky enough to get screened, a short interview ensues and a quick blood sample is taken to make sure your blood is safe. After an hour, the candidate is notified if they can donate. All in all, I feel that the responsibilities of a cuidadore and being a blood donor are extreme commitments to ask even the closest of friends.

Seguro Popular is the other public health insurance in

Mexico, but it is not the same as IMSS. Seguro Popular is a nation-wide healthcare program that is designed as a safety net to cover citizens who are not enrolled or otherwise covered by the IMSS. The service is intended to ensure that all Mexicans, regardless of their socio-economic status, have access to some healthcare. It's most often used by Mexicans who are not in formal employment and cannot afford the IMSS subscriptions. It is possible for foreigners to enroll, as long as they can prove their permanent residency status. However, Seguro Popular is for the poorest of the poor population, individuals and families who have almost nothing. It is a federal program, but runs on monies from the state. IMSS and Seguro Popular are public healthcare options. But, if I used either one of them, I'd have to find cuidadores and blood donors amongst my expat friends. Although it may be possible, it's not feasible. Private insurance is my better option, and one I'm presently researching.

Mexico has a wide range of insurance companies that, for a monthly premium, provide private health coverage. In private hospitals service is much different than with public. Everything is 'laid-on' and billed to the account. As in the states, how much is covered depends on what health care plan is purchased.

I met a dear soul on one of the Facebook groups during my planning year and she became a member of my tribe. Pat has lived here several years and always gives very good advice. She suggests that the three most important things to do when a person first arrives in Lakeside are to obtain a good doctor, a dependable driver, and a Notaria Publica. The latter is an attorney with at least five years' experience who undergoes additional study and apprenticeship before being appointed to Notaria Publica status. The title of a "Notary" north of the border should not be confused with the Notaria Publica of Mexico. They are not the same thing.

When I arrived I immediately secured the doctor and the driver. I have in mind the Notaria Publica I'd like to secure as well. His office is right around the corner from me. I'm still in the process of completing my Mexican Health Care Directive. It is the simplest legal document I can create here in which I state: which persons can make decisions about my health care when I can no longer do it myself. Post life wishes can be included in a Health Care Directive as well. Therein I can express my wishes regarding everything that I wish to happen with my body after I die.

In Chapter 2 I mentioned my transportation and relocation protection plan, where if I transition while across the border, the company (a separate entity from my policy) will arrange to have me or my ashes brought back to Georgia which is my home base. That information is also included within my Health Care Directive. It is an extremely important document which will stay on file with my Notaria Publica and with the Lake Chapala Post Life/Emergency Registry.

I have always made it a point to have my annual physical exams around my birthday in February. Two months after arriving Lakeside I was approaching my birthday. I came across my doctor serendipitously. It was a pull, an unction in my spirit that led me to walk into her office that day. We struck up a conversation, in English and I made an appointment to return for a physical. When I returned I brought the results from my last physical, and she took my family history, vitals and weight. A complete blood work script was written to take to a nearby bio lab once I had properly fasted. She was now my doctor and if the results of the blood work raised any concerns, she would be in contact with me. My birthday is coming around in a few months, so

I'll be stopping in to see her for my yearly physical. I have also seen a dentist since arriving for a routine exam and teeth cleaning. It was a very pleasant experience. Unfortunately, I have some cavities that need filling. Thus far, I've had one filled. It was $45 US dollars. My plan is to get one filled a month until all is resolved. I wear glasses and have two pair; one is for computer use and the other is for everyday use. The prescriptions for my glasses are two years old. It will be time to get an eye exam and new glasses soon. There are an adequate number of optometrists Lakeside to choose from so I'll do the research, check out the reviews, choose one and make an appointment. I was very conscious of putting devices in place to assist me in case I am rendered incapacitated for whatever reason. The fact that I'm in a foreign country alone, doing so was essential. I carry a laminated 5 x 7 index card with me at all times. In Spanish it says my name, address, doctor's name and phone number and the name and number of the person Lakeside to contact in case of an emergency. That person has the names and contact information of my immediate family in the states. This is me, attempting to cover all bases for emergency situations while living abroad.

**Consider your options for healthcare thoroughly when planning and preparing to live abroad.** Finding the best and most affordable healthcare coverage can be daunting. It can also be quite confusing. This is an instance where extensive research is warranted. Don't assume anything; there are always exceptions to the rule. Consider private verses public healthcare. Also, consider finding an attorney sooner rather than later to put in place a legal document that specifies your wishes as it pertains to healthcare directives such as DNR and organ donation.

# Chapter Seven

# Consider: Transportation

I don't have a car. When I first decided to move to Mexico, I intended to pack my 2007 Chevy Cobalt, attach a small trailer, and drive across the border. I researched the actual drive to the Laredo, Texas border crossing from Jonesboro, Georgia. The 17-hour drive seemed doable. I visualized driving towards the border as if it was a work day with two 4- hour shifts and a lunch break in between. Then I would stop for the night and do it all over again the next day. No rush, no stress just taking my time driving to my new home in Mexico. Once I crossed the border it would be an 11-hour drive to my town near Lake Chapala. I also researched what size trailer would be suitable for my small car to pull. Finding a trailer was proving to be a challenge, and more expensive than I had imagined. I would also have to have a hitch installed which carried its own set of issues and costs. I learned that I could bring my US plated car into Mexico if I had a temporal visa, but not with a permanent visa. During this time, I had not yet been to the consulate. I was still of the mindset that I was going to try for a temporal visa. There are couples who both qualify for permanent visas but opt for one of them to obtain a temporal visa just so they can bring and keep their car at least for the four years before the temporal must be turned into a permanent visa. I began reading across several threads in my Facebook groups how murderous the cobblestone streets were on cars that sat low, which mine did. My research on bringing my car across the border started turning up a multitude of rules and regulations that had my mind swirling trying to keep track.

I understood that to drive my car and attached trailer across the border I would need a Temporary Importation Permit (TIP). I could acquire that once I got to the border. The documents needed would be:

✓ Proof of car ownership
✓ Proof of American registration
✓ An affidavit from any lien holders authorizing temporary importation
✓ A valid American driver's license
✓ Proof of citizenship

The list wasn't difficult to follow, but I would need the originals plus two copies of all the documents listed above. I planned on paying my car off before I left, so instead of the affidavit I would need the title. The cost of the TIP wasn't bad. It was the cost of the deposit that gave me pause. The Mexican government requires a deposit plus a one-time only processing fee of $30 to guarantee that your vehicle is returned to the U.S. The deposit would be refunded in cash at the Banjercito office located at the border, if I was to leave Mexico within the authorized period. That period would be 6 months with a tourist visa and within 4 years with a temporal visa. The date the car was manufactured dictates how much the deposit will be. For me, all costs would be times two because the trailer would be treated as another vehicle. The costs for a guarantee deposit were:

• Manufactured **before** 1996 = $200 deposit
• Manufactured **between** 1996 and 2000 = $300 deposit
• Manufactured **after** 2001 = $400 deposit

During the time of researching how to cross with my car and small attached trailer, I had to consider what would happen after my temporal visa (which at the time I was hoping to get) expired after four years, and the permanent visa was issued. I would be left with two choices, either I could nationalize my car or drive it back across the border to try and sell it. The requirements are strict. The types of vehicles allowed to be nationalize are vehicles with capacity for up to 15 passengers (cars, SUVs, pickups, or vans) manufactured in North America. The first digit of the vehicle identification number (VIN) indicates where the vehicle was manufactured, it must be a 1,2,3,4 or 5. Nationalizing my 2007 Chevy Colbalt would cost more than the car was worth. It was something like a 10% import tax, a 16% valued added tax (IVA), and an agent fee. It became very clear to me that unlike applying for my visa, which I did myself, nationalizing my car was not the type of task I could do alone. By law, I would have to hire a customs agent (called an agente aduanal) to handle the whole process for me and pay him for the pleasure of doing so.

If I didn't elect to nationalize, I would have to make an eleven-hour drive to cross the border and sell my car. Then I would have to find a way back to town. The maneuvering of it all this was extremely unappealing to me. The final straw that helped me make the decision not to bring my car was when I learned about what happens at the border crossing into Mexico with an enclosed cargo trailer. First, I would have to make a detailed catalog list both in English and Spanish of my goods, including a description and value. There would be a 50/50 chance that I would be asked to unload the entire trailer, so all items could be inspected. I would then have to load it back; they don't do it for you. I would then be given a form and directed to a window where I would pay a duty tax.

During the time I was researching and trying to decide if I wanted to drive my car into Mexico, an incident occurred which made the thought of **not** having a car, paying for insurance, dealing with maintenance and driving very appealing to me.

It was a warm sunny day, and I had an appointment across town. As I entered the garage I noticed my front left tire was low again. I made a mental note that there was a slow leak in that tire and I was going to have to stop band-aiding it by filling it with air every few days. Pulling out of my driveway, I looked down at the gas gage and noticed I was on just a fourth of a tank. I needed to fill up. No problem, I'd stop at the gas station right before hitting the freeway. I pulled up to pump #1 and proceeded into the gas station where I asked the cashier for $20 dollars on #1 and change for a dollar, explaining to her that I needed to put air in my tire. She obliged, and I walked out, got into my car and drove over to the air pump. After putting in an adequate amount of air, (I knew because I used a gauge), I got back in my car and drove off. While driving down the freeway to my appointment I look down at my gas gage and noticed it was still on a fourth of a tank. Damn! Replaying the whole scene in my mind I realized that I never pumped my gas! I must have been so focused on putting air in my tire I completely blanked out on pumping the gas. Oh well, I was too far down the freeway and closer to my appointment to go back. I reasoned that I had enough gas to get to the appointment and I'd return to the gas station after wards to rectify the situation.

I forged ahead. Thankfully, the appointment was an in and out deal and I was on the freeway heading back to the gas station within an hour. It was still a warm and sunny day as I pulled back in to the gas station, and coincidentally pump #1 was open. I pulled up to it, got out and put the pump inside the tank. I remembered thinking that I should have done it this way in the first place, and maybe that way I wouldn't have forgotten to pump. I walked back into the station where the same cashier was tending to another customer. When my turn came I stepped up and explained how silly I felt but when I paid for my gas, I drove off and never pumped it. She looked at me indifferently and said that there was nothing she do about that. Surely, she hadn't quite understood what I said. So, I explained that it had been less than two hours since I was there. "Remember? I asked." I was the one who asked for change to put air in my tire. I had given her a twenty-dollar bill and a dollar in exchange for four quarters. She then angrily said, "That's not my problem, people can say anything, and you don't have any proof that you didn't pump the gas." Now, I'm blown away and my voice is raised as I say to her the proof is in my #$#@! empty tank! I tried to reason with her, explaining that it made no sense that I would come back and try to get $20 **more** dollars' worth of gas that my tank couldn't hold in the first place. I wanted the gas that I paid for! "And you know I paid for it!" I said.

As we are going back and forth a gentleman standing behind me raises his voice and says, "Man, you know this lady paid for her gas, quit trippin' and give me $10 on #7" as he reached over me to drop a ten-dollar bill through the slot. She takes his money and looks at me like, "This conversation is over." At this point I am totally livid and thoroughly outdone. I started looking around the gas station with the thought, oh you're going give me $20 dollars' worth of something. There were stacks of t-shirts for sale sitting in bins under the large counter. Without thinking any further, I picked up as many of the t-shirts as I could hold, smirked at the cashier and briskly walked five steps to dash out the door. The cashier pushed a button as she stood behind the thick plexiglass protection barrier, and locked me in. I turned to her and demanded she open the door. She picked up the phone and said she was calling the police. I walked over dropped the t-shirts back in the bin and said, "What are you going tell them? That I was gonna steal?" Defeated, I walked back to the door, rattled it and again demanded that she open the door. She ignored me, while holding the phone to her ear.

In a split second I heard the door click as if to open, I spotted a huge incense display sitting on a counter right at the edge of the door (I happen to love incense and burn it daily) in a snap decision I snatched up the display with both hands and bolted out the door. The guy who was in line behind me was pumping his gas, and immediately summarized what had just happen. He looked at me and said, "Oh! You better hurry up." The adrenaline coursing through my veins in that moment was something I had never experienced. I had never done anything like that in my life. I opened my car door, tossed the display in the passenger seat, started the car and shot out of the gas station like a bat out of hell. In that instant I thought I heard a thump of some sort but with the adrenaline on full blast I discarded the thought as soon as it appeared as my tires burned rubber onto the street. I was one exit up from my home, so I dashed onto the freeway breathing heavy as if I had run a hundred-yard dash.

A car pulled up alongside of me on the freeway and when I looked over he was motioning towards the back of my car. I instantly thought the gas cap must be opened. It wouldn't be the first time someone motioned and mouthed to me that fact. I mouthed to him the words gas cap shaking my head in affirmation. He shook his head "no" vigorously. I looked through my side mirror back at the tank and discovered I was dragging the entire gas pump down the freeway! That thump I heard was the pump being snatched out its station. I flashed back to putting the pump in my tank before I had walked back into the station to claim my $20 dollars' worth of gas, assuming that there wouldn't be a problem. Boy, was I wrong! I watched in horror as the sparks were popping off the pump being dragged by my car down the freeway. I came to my exit, pulled over and quickly pulled the pump out from my tank. I threw it over in the grass on the off ramp. I shook my head, got back in my car and drove home. I backed into my garage, let the door down, took a few deep breaths and the incense display I snatched off the shelf invaded my nostrils. I looked down at the gas gage which was just about on empty now, cut the car off, picked up my display of incense and went in the house.

Throughout the rest of that warm and sunny day, I retold the story to family and friends who thought that was one of the funniest stories they'd ever heard. There was teasing, laughing, the asking for boxes of incense, and little concern for police involvement. I never returned to that gas station during the rest of my stay before I moved to Mexico. I'm currently two months away from my one-year anniversary here, and as I write this, I'm burning the incense that was my retribution for not receiving the $20 dollars' worth of gas on that warm and sunny day.

Truly, I had become exhausted with the whole idea of the long hours of driving that would ensue, the eventual costly nationalizing, the listing, the possible crossing to resale, and the abundance of paperwork. I realized the town I was moving to has most everything I would need within walking distance of my rental, or it would be a short bus ride. I have driven and been in possession of a car for over thirty years. I have driven in some of the worse seasons and traffic in Detroit, Las Vegas, and especially Atlanta. I have ridden the waves of high gas prices, had my share of fender benders, maintenance issues and traffic/parking tickets though out those years. Another form of liberation was at hand. I sold my car to the Mexican family next door a week before I departed. Besides, I had a multitude of choices for transportation in Mexico. I could walk, catch a bus, taxi or Uber if the need ever arose. People say "Never say never," but I would be perfectly fine never owning another vehicle in my life.

Although I'm an animal lover, I didn't have the experience of bringing one across the border. However, I feel it is good information and fits well within this chapter on transportation. The consensus I derived after researching travel requirements for pets crossing the border was that traveling to Mexico with a pet is easy. One would need the proper paperwork to enter the country, and it is possible that a pet could undergo an inspection upon arrival at the border or through customs.

All animals crossing the border into Mexico will require the following:

- Duplicate copies of a **health certificate** issued by a licensed veterinarian
- Health certificate must include:
- the name and address of the owner
- physical description of the pet
- must state that the animal is free of any contagious disease
- Vaccinations for rabies and distemper (dates of vaccination must appear on the **health certificate and are time sensitive**)
- Application (can be downloaded at https://bringfido.com)

It's possible that a pet could be quarantined. Healthy pets with proper paperwork do not need to be quarantined in Mexico. Pets are subject to inspection upon arrival, and if they appear ill further examinations by a licensed veterinarian may be required. Documentation appears to be key for an easy crossing. It was also recommended that one should start to prepare documentation and inoculations at least one month before crossing.

**Consider your transportation needs when planning and preparing to live abroad.** How do you see yourself getting around? Thoroughly research the area you are considering and the means of public transportation. Consider living as centrally as you can if you decide not to bring your car. If you bring your car, consider how it is tied to your visa and the time frame in which you can drive a foreign plated car. Consider insurance, maintenance, and even traffic laws. The laws will be different from the US. There's a saying here in Mexico, that stop signs are just suggestions. Having a vehicle verses not having one is a personal decision based on individual lifestyles. Not having one, fits my lifestyle. It was a good decision.

# Chapter Eight

# Consider: Family & Friends

I'm the youngest of three and the only girl. My mom was a single parent, finally found love again and remarried when I was 17 years old. She's 82 years old at the writing of this book, and my step-dad is 96 years old. One brother is a minister and now sits in the pulpit of the church where my mother raised us and has attended for over 50 years. My eldest brother lives in Atlanta and has always been one of my biggest cheerleaders. Two years after my divorce, I made the move from Detroit to Las Vegas. I had just completed my first year as principal at a new charter school that opened under my leadership. The charter management company did not renew my contract after that first year, which was devastating for me.

I needed a clean slate and fresh start. Las Vegas was exploding with growth in 2002, building 10-12 schools a year and desperately seeking teachers to fill them. With a decent severance package, an interview lined up, and a signing bonus when hired, I relocated to Las Vegas. My children were 8 and 11 years old. My kids and I built a wonderful life for ourselves, each of us creating memories and lifetime friendships. I was 50 years old when my youngest went off to college. I woke up one day and felt free enough to start the next chapter in my life. I moved to Atlanta, Georgia. I had family there, my cousin whom I had grown up with in Detroit eagerly awaited my arrival, and we could pick up where we had left off before she got married and moved away. For four great years I lived, built, and created a life with strong connections that I still hold dear today. Georgia is my home base, it's where I hold my US address and where I vote. It's where I retired from teaching and where my son and brother live. My stateside travels include Atlanta, Detroit, Las Vegas, and Salem, Oregon where my daughter, her husband and my grandson live. Travel times by plane for my stateside visits are:

- Atlanta (3 1/2 hours)
- Detroit (6 1/2 hours)
- Las Vegas (3 1/2)
- Salem, Oregon (5 hours)

Traveling to all those locations and staying from one to two weeks in each place can be expensive, so trips stateside are strategically planned. The only trips set in stone for me are Oregon for my grandson's birthday, and Detroit for my mother's. Holiday's will generally be spent in Mexico. I'm looking forward to family and friends, son and eventually daughter visiting me here in Mexico. My cousin has already made a visit. She was the first, and hopefully more will follow.

Striking out on my own and moving abroad was a **"me"** decision. It didn't include input from family or friends. Opinions were not sought. The decision began and ended with me. I was in total control of my own life, had retired, my kids were grown, and I was single. I had absolutely no attachments to negotiate or really consider. It had been over 15 years since I moved away from my hometown of Detroit. I'm my mother's only daughter and it did give pause until recalling what my mom told me in 2015.

I had just retired and spent the summer with my mom

trying to convince her to downsize her house and move to an assisted living facility where her and Pop could liberate themselves of homeownership and be (I assumed) more comfortable. I was met with a great deal of resistance and told I should let her be and leave that subject alone. My mom told me she had my brother, the minister, and his four grown children, who checked on them and their needs regularly, and that she was absolutely fine.

Although I didn't know it at the time, the assurances she gave me that day, allowed me to envision myself living abroad much easier. There were a lot of questions that I couldn't answer when I began making my announcement, so when I was bombarded with questions, I simply said, "I'm in the research stage." That seemed to appease everyone and deter questions that I wasn't ready to or couldn't answer. During that year of planning and preparing I was left alone mostly to do just that. As I became more sure of certain aspects of the move I disclosed that information to those who needed to know.

My mother was very ill during the time that I started wrapping up my research and was in full swing of planning and preparing. I made the conscious decision not to tell her. I made a public plea on Facebook to family and friends who are in contact with her not to tell her. She was battling colon cancer, COPD, Crohn's disease, diabetes, and high blood pressure. My mom is a worrier by nature and at 81 years old I wasn't about to add any stress to her already full plate. She needed to focus on getting healthy, not her only daughter moving to Mexico. Everyone obliged and the secret was kept. My cousin was looking for a bigger place and moved into my house a few months before I left it. I did tell mom I was moving to a smaller more manageable condo because I didn't need all the space the current house provided, and my cousin did. My mother was going to think I was still in Atlanta, and with my cell phone number popping up when I called her, she wouldn't be the wiser. So, when I first moved to Mexico my mom was under the impression that I still lived in Georgia. Family and friends helped to cover for me, understanding it was in her best interest not to know.

Once I moved and began settling in and meeting new friends, I would mention from time to time that my mom didn't know I lived in Mexico. Boy, did they think that was a hoot. I would explain why and they, like many back in the states, understood my logic. I was in Mexico acclimating quite well for five months before I returned stateside for what wound up being a monumental milestone kind of visit. It started in Atlanta. Once there I had to purchase several new outfits because I had lost over twenty pounds in those first five months abroad. That felt good. I also had to pick up hair care products, get my hair cut, and hang out with my cousin. Then it was on to Detroit, I was to be a bridesmaid in my oldest niece's wedding. I was going to be there for a week. Once I arrived, I went straight to the boutique where the bridesmaid dress was waiting for me. It had to be taken in quite a bit as well. My niece was getting married on a Saturday, and the next day was Mother's Day. I was happy I could be there for both events but reminded family and friends to keep my secret because mom had had her surgery and was recovering quite well. It wasn't the time to reveal such a secret.

The next stop during my stateside visit was to my daughter in Salem, Oregon, who was expecting her first child. The baby wasn't due until the 21st of May. I was flying in on the 14th to be there for the delivery. However she had the baby on the 9th and was home with my grandson three days before I arrived. When she and my son-in-law picked me up from the airport my first grandbaby was in the car and a whole new love affair began. I stayed with my daughter for two and a half months, helping out while she healed from her C-section surgery. I was in the states for three and a half months in total. During that time, I sent my rent via Western Union.

A few weeks before I was to leave Salem, I discovered that my mother had created a Facebook account and was friend requesting family members including me! She had recovered fully from her surgery and all other ailments were in check. She had lots of time on her hands to figure out the basics and she did. I had documented my move to Mexico, and if she continued down my timeline she would discover that is indeed where I actually lived. Fortunately, I had been in the states for the past three months and since I post regularly she would definitely have to dig deep into my timeline to discover the secret. But it became apparent to me as she grew in her social media aptitude daily that I was going to have to own up to the secret before I crossed the border. My mom was 82 years old and I didn't see that coming. I never saw her getting a Facebook account. For so many years she called it "the devil."

I made my way back through Atlanta for a week before heading home. It was my son's 28th birthday weekend and I was excited to spend it with him. Before I departed for Mexico, I had a phone call to make. I needed to tell my mom that I lived in Mexico. The actual conversation is a blur to me now but I remember explaining that she was sick and how I wanted her to focus on getting well and not worry about me. I remember her saying she had already known and she was disappointed that I felt that I couldn't tell her the truth. She was real salty about the lie and let me know. I knew that it was going to take some time for her to be okay with everything, and to date we're still rather tip-toeing with the entire idea of it all. Facebook helps because she gets to see that all is well and I'm involved in an active expat community and living my best life.

I'm an extrovert. Meeting new people and making friends has always been pretty easy for me. Case in point, I had been here two full months by the time my 55th birthday rolled around. I threw myself a birthday party on the rooftop of a local bar and had close to 30 of my dearest friends in attendance. Several of those friends were people in my hiking group.

While north of the border planning and preparing, I had been following a very active hiking group on Facebook in the area. I was fascinated with the beautiful pictures they would post on the group's site. The people posting seemed really nice. I took an interest, having never hiked a day in my life, and I had made up my mind while north of the border that I would try it out once I arrived and settled in. I must have started hiking some time in December because when I look back at my calendar, January 2018 was full of checks (which meant I did it) on Tuesdays and Fridays, which are the official hiking group's, hike days. People are free to hike the mountains anytime they want, and some do, forgoing the morning meeting where each hike is described, before taking off with the hike group of your choice. I met some of the most fascinating people from all over the world. There's nothing like coming together with a group of people for a common goal, to get to the top of the mountain and back down safely. This is done all while listening to and participating in great conversation and breathtaking views, not to mention an excellent way to exercise.

One day on a hike someone mentioned how yoga was an

excellent form of stretching and how it helps with coordination and balance, which hikers need. There is a yoga studio a couple blocks from me, so I signed up and started taking beginners yoga on Mondays, Wednesdays, and Thursdays which were the days I didn't hike. I absolutely love yoga; the connection I make with my body while practicing is amazing. I've learned the importance of breath work through yoga. Meditation soon followed, and I began to experience a wonderful mind, body and soul connection. It's really easy to meet people Lakeside if you're open. Especially someone like me who sticks out in a crowd. I'm Black, with reddish/blondish hair, and my name is Queen. There are not many Black people residing Lakeside. I can count us on my hands. I have spent the majority of my years within the Black community and honestly didn't have any White friends that I socialized with outside of work until I moved here. This is different for me. In most situations, events and gatherings I am the only Black in attendance. However, I find the mindsets of the majority of expats here are that of acceptance, not tolerance. I have not experienced any form of racism here. If there are racist here they don't go out of their way to expose themselves as such. I do have a few Black girlfriends around my age here. It's always a treat when I get together with my "sistahs" south of the border for lunch, dinner or a local event because there are so few of us here, and we're pretty spread out throughout Lakeside.

I'm often asked if I'm dating or if there is a dating pool within the community where I live. My answer is no to both questions. I understood before moving here that dating would probably be nonexistent for me. It was not a consideration that carried any weight when making my decision. Everyone is different. Dating and an adequate dating pool would definitely be a determining factor for some. As it relates to dating, I feel everyone has their own unique preferences. My personal preference is not a demographic here. My life in Mexico is full, stress-free and rich with various social events and activities.

**Consider your family and friends when planning and preparing to live abroad.** You hold a unique position within your family. Most people are extremely attached to their involvements. Some are lifelong members in fraternal organizations, churches, community activities, and social groups. Those entanglements can be very hard to detach from and much consideration should be given to whether one could really handle that type of separation. Consider the hours it will take to fly home in case of an emergency. For me personally a 16-hour flight home was a deterrent. My family is spread out across the US and the longest flight to an immediate family member is six hours. Here's a good time to do a self-check, on any separation issues within your family, especially your kids. I was very fortunate in that my two grown kids were doing well adulting in their own right and were proud of this bold move I was making for myself. Consider your racial proclivity, especially if dating is a strong factor within your lifestyle. Chances are in most countries you will be a minority, and you won't see a lot of your ethnicity, especially if you're Black, in your country of choice. This is yet another opportunity to do a self-check, to examine your feelings about that issue. Consider investing in and bringing with you whatever you need to keep you healthy and happy for your mind, body and soul. Also consider holding an address in the states possibly with a family member. You are still a US citizen. You just happen to reside in another country.

# Chapter Nine

## Consider: Communication

I lost my cell phone six days after arriving at Lakeside. When I arrived I only had two suitcases which held some clothes and toiletries, I was in good shape though because my rental was completely furnished. My personal things, thanks to my Mexican family next door, would be arriving from the states in a few days. I absolutely loved my condo; it was perfect for me. It was a cozy, safe, centrally located nest that I would turn into a sanctuary once my things arrived. It was just awaiting my final touches to make it a home. In the meantime, I needed to go grocery shopping and start cooking some meals for myself. That sun-drenched afternoon, I started the ten-minute walk to Walmart. I was feeling pretty proud of myself because I was settling in so well. My plan was to shop and take a taxi back. I had noticed that a few always seemed to be stationed off to the side of the front doors. Shopping took a while because I was still learning labels, converting prices from dollars to pesos on my app, figuring out where things were, all while face-timing with my daughter. We were having a good ol' time on the phone laughing and talking as I showed her different labels and products in Spanish. The Walmart in my new town was very different from the Walmart I was use to in the states. Items that I thought would be next to each other were in a totally different area. Take for instance flushable wipes; usually they are near the toilet paper, right? I found them in the aisle with deodorant. In many instances, there doesn't seem to be any rhyme or reason, and items appear where they appear. I just had to look very carefully or use Google translate when I had to ask a worker, as language was a barrier.

I hung up with my daughter while standing in the checkout line. Shopping complete, I stepped outside and began looking around. There are men who wash cars in the parking lot while you shop. That's one of the many jobs I see here that speaks to the ingenuity and strong work ethic that Mexicans have. One of the parking lot car washers, gestured to me and said, "Taxi?" I nodded and he waved a taxi over to where I stood by the front door. The gentleman got out and loaded my groceries in the trunk while I settled into the back seat. When the driver pulled up to my gate, I realized that I didn't have my remote to open it. I explained I had to go get it and would open the gate from the inside. He simply nodded. I don't know if he understood me or not. I grabbed my purse, used my key to walk through the door-gate portion to my complex, retrieved my remote and opened the gate. My place is located maybe 25 steps from the entry gate and I was standing outside my door so the driver could see me. He pulled right up, popped his trunk, got out, and helped bring the groceries inside. I was trying to figure the tip in pesos for the $70 peso ($3.00 US) taxi ride up the street. I figured $20 pesos ($1.00 US). I paid him, and he made his turn around in the complex and honked as he passed my door. I looked out and he pointed to the gate. Oh! I needed to let him out. I picked up the remote, clicked the button and he drove out. I walked back inside and commenced putting my groceries away. I situated a few items and begin looking for my phone. I checked my purse, through all the grocery bags, counter, table top, and pockets. Mentally retracing steps, I asked myself when was the last time I had it? Looked at it? OH MY GOD!! It hit me like a ton of bricks, I had left my cell phone in the back seat of the taxi! I immediately started panicking, pacing the floor and shouting NO! NO! NO! I would have to walk back to Walmart! I grabbed my keys and purse, locked the door and headed out.

I had recently met my next door neighbors, Sue and her husband Willie. Both were in their early 80's, snowbirds who drove down from Canada. We had met and spoken a few times in the six days since my arrival. As I passed her door they were sitting in their screened-in front porch, working crossword puzzles. Practically in tears I explained to her I left my cell phone in the back of the taxi, that he hadn't been gone too long and I needed a ride back up to Walmart to catch him. She saw the panicked look on my face and agreed to take me back to Walmart. She moved so slowly, finding the keys, walking to their car, starting the engine, pulling out of the parking space, using the remote to open the gate, and pulling out into traffic. It was agonizing, painful, distressing and the slowest process ever! We finally made it into the parking lot and she pulled up a little ways from the front door. I just jumped out and went over to the group of car washers. I asked the group as best I could with my limited Spanish, for the taxi driver who just took me home. I went on to explain, using hand motions, that I had left my cell phone in the back seat. This was the first time I was experiencing a communication barrier and I was damn near hysterical by now. I needed my phone! Fortunately there were a couple men in the group who understood me and asked for my phone number to call my phone. Another man appeared to know who I was talking about and he started calling the taxi driver. There was no answer each time they called. My heart sunk deeper into my stomach and my eyes welled up with tears. Eventually, I was standing there in front of those men as people walked by crying out loud like a baby. I couldn't help it. It was humiliating, I was scared, six days into this foreign country, not speaking the language well, all alone and I didn't have my phone.

After what seem like an eternity, the taxi driver finally answered his phone. He said he had taken another rider not far and was on his way back. I was told that he also stated that he hadn't seen or heard a phone ringing and he didn't pick up his own phone because he was driving. He pulled up several minutes later and I walked over along with the two English speaking car washers. The driver stepped out and went through a dramatic display of searching for my phone, he even folded the back seat forward so we could look underneath. The phone was gone. There was nothing I could do about it. Defeated, I walked back to Sue's car and got in. I told her that retrieval efforts had failed. I was now numb, with no words to speak. Sue, asked me why would I take my phone with me? Why wouldn't I leave it at home? I attributed that question to her age, and solemnly agreed that I should have left it at home. I thanked her for taking me back up to Walmart and waiting during the whole ordeal. When I entered my place, I broke down. I didn't have my personal things, and I didn't have my phone. In that moment I felt extremely disconnected and alone in the world. I'm a pacer when stressed and while pacing back and forth I recognized my tablet on my nightstand. I had Wi Fi already hooked up and immediately jumped on Facebook and cried out that I had lost my phone, and wasn't sure what to do. Within minutes my daughter called me on Facebook messenger. I was so happy to hear her voice and to know I wasn't cut off from the world like I was imagining. She asked me did I have lock on my phone. I didn't. Therefore, my banking information was front and center. All someone had to do was click on the Chase or Capital One icon and they would have access to my debit and credit card info. After scolding me for not having a lock she performed a three-way call to each bank, so that I could deactivate the accounts. Accomplishing that part gave me a sense of security. I ordered new cards to be sent to my Atlanta home base address. My cousin would overnight the cards once they arrived. I took a deep breath, and slowly began to realize, that I would survive the ordeal and that besides being inconvenienced, I would be alright. Everything would be alright. I could still communicate via my tablet, new cards were ordered, my things were still on the way, and precious pictures could be retrieved via Google Cloud. I now was going to have to get a Mexican cell phone much sooner than I anticipated.

The ability to communicate is vital when living abroad. I was very fortunate to have my tablet when I lost my cell phone. When my things arrived I had my laptop as well. I communicate over several platforms. I have a cell phone, tablet, and laptop. Most times when communicating with my inner circle of family and friends I use Facebook messenger, and video chat. It's convenient because the platform allows for group or individual calls, texts and video chats for free. Nothing gives my heart more pleasure than to get both my kids on video chat. We laugh, chat, and show the goings on in our domains. What's really cool now is my first grandchild, my son's first nephew is present and an added bonus to our family chats. When my daughter calls me it's mostly on Facebook video chat and she always leads with my grandson's beautiful face appearing on my phone screen as the first thing I see. To push the green phone symbol and see his face pop up, toothless and grinning from ear to ear, is so cool, it gives me life.

I rely on Wi Fi quite a bit here in Mexico. It's very common to go to a restaurant, doctor or dentist office, salon, bar or a friend's home and ask for the Wi Fi passcode. I only use my data like most people Lakeside, when I cannot attach to Wi Fi. Whatsapp and IMO are two other apps I use the same way that I use Facebook. I can call, text and video chat for free on those apps as well. Many times I use Whatsapp. It's a common platform for businesses, drivers, and local contacts Lakeside. I talk to my kids, cousin, and close friend in Las Vegas daily. We all pretty much fell in to a routine of sorts, because of the time differences I talk to my cousin on her lunch break which is 11:00 am my time. I talk to my Las Vegas friend on her lunch break which is 3:00 pm my time, and my kids call anytime they are so inclined and I just better pick up, or multiple calls take place back to back to back. It's a good system because if they don't talk to me within a day, they have phone numbers of my tribe members and landlord to request a well check if necessary. Because communication within my inner circle is daily, the fact that I am in another country instead of another state is a non-factor.

I am extremely thankful for the free readily available platforms that I use to communicate. Phoning while in Mexico can be tricky. What I dial depends on the type of phone I'm **using** and the type of phone I'm **calling** (landline or mobile). I became aware of this when I saw an actual flow chart of "How to dial" during my research. Calling to the U.S. and Canada is fairly easy, I just dial 001 + Area Code + phone number. My friends and family numbers are set up that way in my Mexican cell phone. It gets tricky with Toll Free calls to the U.S. or Canada because there is no such thing as a Toll Free call and regular long distance rates apply. It's the "instead" that's intricate:

- For toll numbers starting with 880 **instead** dial 866
- For toll numbers starting with 800 **instead** dial 880
- For toll numbers starting with 877 **instead** dial 882
- For toll numbers starting with 888 **instead** dial 881

How to dial a Mexican cell phone compared to a Mexican landline can be quite dicey as well. To call a Mexican cell phone from the U.S. first dial the International Code **(011)**, + the Country Code **(52)** + **(1)** then the 10 digit Mexican number. That's a total of 16 numbers! To call a Mexican cell phone from a Lakeside land line first dial **(045)** + Area Code **(376)** + then the 10 digit Mexican number. I find most locals communicate with expats and each other via Whatsapp. I have a landline with a phone number that's connected to the Wi Fi modem but I never use it, nor does it ever ring. To call a Mexican land line from the U.S. first dial the International Code **(011)**, + the Country Code **(52)** + Area Code **(376)** then the seven digit local number.

I'm often asked how I receive my mail. The answer is, I don't. All important business that needs to be conducted (which is not much when you are retired) is handled through email. Mail is not handled the traditional way it is in the states. There is no mail person with a specified route or a truck, nor is there a mailbox attached to your residence for mail. There are, however, business centers that operate as a post office. Residents can pay a fee for the use of a mailbox like they would in the states. Entities such as FedEx, UPS and DHL, run through the center daily with deliveries and pickups. I could and have had packages delivered to the center located a block from my rental. It cost a very minimal fee to retrieve a package. However, it is very costly to mail packages in and out of Mexico. I am aware that some, mostly homeowners do indeed have packages delivered directly to their home without issue. People shop Amazon and Amazon MX and can have their items delivered to a business center as well. There is also a mail service for the Lake Chapala Society members. Volunteer LCS members traveling north will drop postage in a mail box in the United States. Their service desk even has U.S. postage stamps for sale. Then there's the expat "muleing" system. I ordered hiking poles from Amazon and had them delivered to a friend in Colorado. When she came down, she brought my poles. When I return to the states, I stocked up on haircare products, creams, soaps, and a particular skin oil that I can't get here. I actually made three trips home during my first year in Mexico, my daughter's baby shower in March, a May-August summer visit that encompassed three states, and an October weekend visit for my cousin's 50th birthday celebration. Each time I made sure to bring back needed products.

Having access to events around the world and relaxing with my favorite television shows from north of the border is essential to my wellbeing. Living in Mexico has not hindered my ability to do either. I brought my 19' smart TV. It was packed along with my laptop, and Firestick. For watching TV in real time, I subscribed to USTV NOW. It's an online service that offers American expats and military personnel a wide range of American channels to watch via computer, tablet, or smart TV. The free subscription only gives me a few channels and somehow, I get Pittsburg's local news. However, the channels I do get allow me to watch my favorite dramas in real time. When I don't catch my shows in real time, which is often, I'll do a catch up binge during my down time using my Firestick. I also have a Netflix subscription for which I pay a monthly $8.00 fee. I've enjoyed several original series with Netflix. Eventually, as the years go by, I'm sure I will purchase Mexican electronics but it was important to me that I kept and operated my north of the border electronics that work well together for the time being.

Music is also essential to my wellbeing. Through my electronics I use several venues to enjoy my north of the border music daily. I brought by blue tooth speaker and aux cord. So whether the aux is hooked up to my phone or tablet I continue to jam through Pandora, iHeart Radio, and my YouTube playlist. Days after arriving, I purchase a Virtual Private Network (VPN) in order to connect to Pandora with all my saved stations. While following threads within the Lakeside Facebook groups I learned about VPN's and the possibility of needing one once I was living south of the border. When I connect to a VPN, I create a secure, encrypted tunnel between my devices and the VPN remote server. It's like the server hides my IP location and my device appears to be located stateside. That's important because without it, if I try and connect to Pandora, it will message that it does not work outside the country. I connect to my VPN and retry and it will then allow for Pandora to open up, no problem. I researched the VPN's I heard mentioned in the group and found a very good one that cost $39.00 for a year subscription. With iHeart Radio, I listen to my favorite radio stations and radio personalities in real time from Detroit and Atlanta. YouTube is vital because it contains various playlists that I've worked hard on over the years. Moving abroad I didn't have to give up what I've come to know, trust and love with television or music. I am still very well connected to family, friends, and current events happening around the world.

**Consider how you will stay connected when planning and preparing to live abroad.** There are various ways to communicate. Consider having more than one device to do so. My laptop was packed away, and if I didn't have my tablet I can't imagine how I would have handled losing my phone just six days after arriving.

It is also advisable to maintain a home base address in the states, one that coincides with your state license. It just makes things like voting, renewing your license, and conducting state business (which you will most likely continue to have) much easier. I was fortunate to maintain the address on my license, because when I moved out of my home in Georgia, my cousin moved in. Therefore, it has remained my home base. My situation is of course unique. I know expats that maintain a mailbox at one of the business centers, and ones who pay for some type of virtual mail assistant. Since that wasn't going to be my case I never researched that possibility.

Consider establishing a phone chain of sorts from stateside to your country abroad upon arriving. Ensure that your inner circle stateside has the number(s) of people who can account for your wellness and whereabouts if necessary until you start building your community of friends wherever you land. My cousin and children were given the number of my landlord. She was my first and only point of contact when I arrived. Gain an understanding for how the phone system works in your chosen country. What is the area code? What is the International code? Are they different when dialing from landlines? Those are the types of questions you should have answered before you go. Also consider, your plan for staying informed in a foreign country. It's important to know how you will watch television or listen to music, because living in a foreign country is quite different and you will need an adequate amount of electronics to ensure you stay informed and entertained using devices and platforms that you are comfortable with when living abroad.

# Chapter Ten

# Consider: A Recon Visit

Reconnaissance means to check out a situation before taking action. It makes good sense to do a "boots on the ground" reconnaissance mission to evaluate as many aspects as possible of your future home. However, that's something I never did before I moved to Las Vegas, Atlanta or Mexico. In Spring of 2002, I found myself at a crossroads in my life. When my contract wasn't renewed after my first year as principal at the Charter Academy, I was devastated. I was 39 years old, divorced with two kids and unemployed. I was in desperate need of a fresh start. I've always been the type of person that received an "all of a sudden" explosion of a crystal-clear thought putting me on a path I never imagined.

For instance, when I was 18 years old, three weeks after graduating high school, I announced to my mom that I had found a place and was moving out. That announcement was the result of me acting upon some very clear thoughts that I was having about living on my own. I've always been extremely independent, and my decease father's social security benefits allowed for me to begin experiencing and experimenting with life as an adult. A year later at the age of 19, I announced that I was moving to Minneapolis, MN to live with my grandmother, which I did for a year and a half.

Another announcement to my family came the Spring of

2002. I announced that my kids and I were relocating to Las Vegas, NV. I didn't know anyone there, nor had I ever been there. But I researched and what I did discovered was that the sun shone 300+ days a year and I needed some sunshine in my life. Clark County School District was hiring teachers at an enormous rate to combat their population explosion and giving signing bonuses to boot. I began searching for a rental, researching the statistics of communities and neighborhoods, preparing for the sale of my home, and reconciling with family that this move was really going to happen. I found a townhome I liked and began conversations with the property manager on site. Through faxes, emails and phone calls I placed a deposit down on our first home in Las Vegas, sight unseen. I had a huge yard sale, hired a moving company and a transportation company to transport my car. On the 28th of June my mom and pop dropped the kids and I off at the airport. We had our suitcases, and I had an address and a pending interview with the District. When we arrived, I hailed a taxi and gave him the address to our place. He dropped us off at the property office and the on-site manager greeted me, finally happy to put a face with the name. She walked us around to our townhome, handed me the keys and I handed her the first month's rent. Days later my car arrived and months later our things finally arrived. I had a horrible experience with the moving company I hired, but I learned a lot in the process. I lived in Las Vegas for eleven years and I raised my kids there. Together we created a life full of community involvements, church, friends, and even family. Unbeknownst to me, my mom had cousins living in Las Vegas and she put me in touch with them. We've been connected ever since. It was a good move; the best move I could have ever made for myself and my kids.

In 2012, my daughter graduated from high school and

was heading to University of Reno that fall. My son had just finished his sophomore year at Christian Brothers University in Memphis, Tennessee. He had made it clear that he was adulting now and wasn't interested in sleeping on the sofa during his summers off. Once he left for college, I downsized to a two bedroom. He was electing to stay with friends and work during his summers off. In February of 2013, I turned 50 years old. An "all of a sudden" explosion of a crystal-clear thought hit again. It was so strong that I shot up in bed and announced to no one in particular, that I was moving to Atlanta, Georgia. This would be my last year teaching in the Clark County School District, I would leave at the end of June. I had lived, worked and raised my kids in Las Vegas for eleven years. My cousin, whom I'm very close to, had been asking me for years to move down to Atlanta. She had married and moved there when our boys were just five years old. We had been inseparable in Detroit, raising our boys together. The thought of being back together with her made me happy. Then came the announcement to my kids, family and friends. My son, who had visited Atlanta for a conference, fell in love with it, and was excited with the idea. My daughter, on the other hand, who had just completed her freshmen year at UNR, was shocked. My suggestion was for her to come with me and transfer colleges. However, she had met and was dating her now husband. They met at Sears where she was working, to help offset her college expenses. It was serious relationship, and she opted to stay in Reno.

I began researching school districts in Georgia. Unlike Las Vegas, where there is one huge school district, Georgia has multiple districts. I started applying in Clayton, Henry, DeKalb, and Fulton (Atlanta) counties. I also started looking for a rental, I was pleasantly surprised at the low rental prices and the amount of space I could get for my money. I didn't want to be too far from where my cousin lived, and I was constantly asking her about one area vs. another. I found a place that I really liked, the rent was exactly what I had been paying for my 2 bedroom, 2 bath townhome in Las Vegas. It was a 3 bedroom, 2 and 1/2 bathroom place with a great room, large front yard with a front porch that ran the length of the house, extra-large fenced-in backyard, attached garage and a long driveway. It was surrounded by trees and situated in the back of a cud de sac, all for $875.00 a month! To top it off, it was one exit up the freeway from my cousin.

As with Las Vegas, I faxed, emailed and made phone calls until I secured that wonderful home by placing a deposit down, again sight unseen. I also made deposits with the utility companies and made sure that they were turned on and in my name once the security deposit was made. School was out for the summer and I could devote my time to packing, donating, and throwing away items that weren't going to make the move. Most of my daughter's valuable things went with her to Reno, as did my son's to Memphis. Anything of value that was theirs, I packed up in a box for them. After packing, I rented a U-Haul, hired a couple day laborers who stand in front of Lowe's or Home Depot early in the morning, and had them pack the truck. I enlisted the help of my son, who was still living in Memphis, to fly home to take the 3-day cross country journey with me to Georgia. He lovingly obliged and arrived in Las Vegas the night before we were to depart the city he and his sister had called home. We were in no hurry, so we made driving an 8-hour day. We'd start in the morning drive 4 hours, stop for lunch, drive another 4 or so hours and grab a motel for the night, then do it all again the next day.

On July 1, 2013, I arrived in Atlanta, Georgia. We drove

up the long driveway as the leasing officer from the Property Management Company stood waiting on the front porch. As the leasing officer walked me around my new home showing and explaining features I was so very pleased with everything my senses were taking in. I signed a few documents then yielded the cashier's check for the first month's rent. He handed me the keys, wished me well, and left. My son had backed the U-Haul in close near the garage and let the hatch up. We stood staring at the job before us when a group of 3 guys and 2 women walked up to us from our left side. I noticed right away that they were Mexican, their faces had big smiles and right away they began introducing themselves and asking if we need any help. I readily accepted, introducing myself and my son. I looked up and the men in the family had already jumped in and started handing down items off the truck.

I remember thinking how nice of them and that this was definitely a good move. I had a peace about it, and finally being back with my cousin was icing on this "moving down south" piece of cake. Unlike when I moved to Las Vegas, I didn't have an interview lined up with any of the Districts where I had applied. I wasn't worried though; it was summer, and I was confident that I'd land a job before the school year started, and I did. I settled in quite nicely to Georgia's slower paced lifestyle and genuine hospitality. My cousin's tribe quickly became mine, I made a few forever friends on my own, and created a host of memories. I lived in Atlanta for four years, my son eventually moved to Atlanta and so did my oldest brother. It's my home base now. After my second year in Georgia, having taught and administrated in Detroit 14 years, and taught in Las Vegas 11 years, I happily retired.

That "all of a sudden" explosion of a crystal-clear thought hit again while I was reading an article on the top ten places to retire and live comfortably. As it happened, I had grown weary of the need to find and keep jobs to supplement my pension and that article resonated with my spirit. After planning and preparing for a year I again put down a deposit on my condo as I had done for Las Vegas and Atlanta, sight unseen. My landlord did do a video walk through, and everything that was in the rental ad, was present in the video. I was again confident enough to send a deposit to hold the place. My friends could attest to my very nature being one of organization and planning, almost to a fault. They make fun of me when it's time for an event, I've been known to take over attempting to instill order as to how things should be.

Yes, I'm obsessed with the order of things. So much so, that I planned out what my first five days would look like once I arrived Lakeside. I spent time on Google Street View walking the street paths to where I was going to go, eat, and shop. I couldn't wait! I was so excited to carry out my plans, while still living north of the border, Mexico was all I thought about. My goal was to settle in immediately upon arriving.

I arrived in Guadalajara by way of Delta Airlines on December 1, 2017, at 1:05pm. My plan was after I cleared customs, I would walk over to the official taxi stand and take a cab to my town, which was a 30-minute ride from the airport. I gathered my two suitcases, got a green light through customs and walked through the large automatic doors. The first sight was overwhelming. There were all these hues of brown people, short, tall, big, and small gathered around waiting for their love ones to come through the doors. I looked to the left and spotted the sign for taxis. I began walking over and I heard a voice calling, "Meeschele, Meeschele, Meeschele" I turned around to see an unassuming man smiling and walking towards me. He said, "I am Manual. We talked on Facebook, and I said I'd pick you up." "I couldn't reach you so I took a chance." I instantly remembered our Facebook conversation. It was around two months prior, I had just bought my plane ticket, and with my obsessive planning I had a conversation with Manual. He is a member in the Dependable Drivers Guadalajara Facebook group, which I went on to secure a driver. I did remember giving him the date and time of my arrival. But, we never connected again, although the conversation had crossed my mind a couple times, I never touch based with him again to confirm. I figured, I'd just catch a taxi. I was delighted that he had remembered and took a chance on me being there, I took it as a sign, a very positive sign. It was a beautiful sunny day, with clear skies and brown mountains. My landlord pulled up to the complex shortly after we did, and I had walked across the street and bought a can of Jack Daniels Honey and Lemonade mix. I remember taking a picture of the can and sending it to my friend in Las Vegas because she buys that mix separately. Here I was, and the first thing I drank south of the border is the combined drink. I was indeed showing off, and I knew she would get a kick out of it.

Just like the property manager in Las Vegas, and the leasing officer in Atlanta my landlord in Mexico showed me around my humble, cozy, just right for me abode. I handed her the first month's rent in pesos and she handed me the keys and the remote to the gate, gave me a hug and left. I was happy with the quaintness and cleanliness of my condo, and also to see it was stocked with basic cleaning supplies. I wiped the bathroom down and unpacked my toiletries, then hung my clothes and took note of what I would need from Walmart.

Around 5 pm I headed out walking to the restaurant

where I had planned to have my first meal south of the border. I had walked there a hundred times on Google Street View and was eager to see the landmarks to guide me on my way. The cobblestone streets are tough to navigate as I had already learned in one of the Facebook groups. As I walked down the street I was filled with joy. I had done it! I was on my way to have my filet mignon "Welcome-to-Mexico" dinner. Feeling confident and accomplished each step I took filled me with joy. Each step until my foot came right out from under me and I fell on my ass! Yes, there were people outside and yes, they saw me fall and quickly bounce my ass back up. I shook my head and told myself, well there's my first fall. I had got that out of the way. I dusted myself off and kept going. My meal was absolutely delicious. I took pictures and posted on Facebook. The cost in pesos for my meal plus two margaritas was equivalent to $14.00 US. I was on cloud nine already going over the plans for day two in my head as I walked home after my first meal.

As I write this I'm a few weeks away from celebrating that very day. I'm closing in on my first year here in Mexico. What have I created in a year? What do my days look like now that I'm settled? I've been able to finally go on a journey of self-discovery, which was easy to do, without the stress and hustle and bustle of the states. I soon began to create what I wanted to experience spiritually, emotionally, physically, mentally, socially, and financially. After taking a free 21 Day Meditation course with Oprah and Deepak, I continued meditating daily. I equate meditation with prayer, I go within and become one with my creator. "God in me, expressed as me and is me" is my spiritual mantra. Through meditation I have reach levels of consciousness and clarity I never imagined. I'm clearer than ever that I am a spiritual being having a human experience in this time/space dimension. I've come to embrace and own my every emotion. I now recognize my emotions for what they are and why I'm experiencing them. I now let the emotion run its course because it doesn't create, but it's an indication of what I'm creating in my time/space reality. My emotions are my guidance system, so that I am in complete control of where I'm going at any given time.

Physically, I am living healthier than I ever did stateside. My core is strong, my skin healthy, and my vitals are reminiscent of my 30's. I went from barely being able to complete the easiest of hikes, to being asked to lead a hike when the actual hike leader was unavailable. I hike twice a week and practice yoga three times a week. I have lost a total of over 30 lbs. as I close out my first year since arriving at Lakeside. I communicate with my body, and I now listen when it communicates with me. My mind is active and strong through reading, writing, coloring, and working puzzles online. I keep my mental state engaged and learning.

Living in Mexico I have met some of the most fascinating people from all over the world. I hike with them, break bread with them, party and converse with them. I have created meaningful and purposeful relationships that support, love and inspire me to live my best life. Financially, I can honestly state that my rent of $500.00 is close to half of the $1,100 pension I get a month. However, because utilities and food are cheap, and I don't own a car, I can literally save $200.00 a month **if** I stick to my budget. I have yet to really save because I like to travel and experience new things. As a teacher, I always desired to inspire my students to love learning, like I did. **Now** that I've moved abroad alone, **now** that I wake up every day with a song in my heart, and **now** that I am healthy in every area of my life I hope to inspire other women. I especially want middle-aged women to know that it's never too late to go on a journey of self-discovery. Whether it leads you abroad or not, self-discovery leads to self-love and self-love leads to you living your best life and highest good.

**Consider doing a reconnaissance visit when planning and preparing to live abroad.** I have moved from Detroit to Las Vegas, Las Vegas to Atlanta, and Atlanta to Mexico. However, for multitude of reasons, I never made a reconnaissance trip beforehand. With all my relocations, I stepped out on faith. I took a leap of faith each time. It felt right in my soul each time. Nevertheless, boots on the ground is a very logical consideration and if you're able, I recommend that you do it. Research the country and find out if there are tours available. I know for Mexico there is a Focus on Mexico organization, searchable on Facebook. It hosts an in-depth 6-day on-the-ground live program in Mexico to provide everything a person would need to know to make a move. Consider planning out your first five days upon arrival. What do those days look like? What are you doing? Where are you going? How will you get there? There are a multitude of questions that must be answered beforehand, because once the plane lands, you are a foreigner in a foreign country. Be smart, be careful, and be patient with yourself and your new country. You chose to move abroad, and I'm sure that decision wasn't made haphazardly. Trust that decision and yourself. Get ready for a journey of self-discovery and adventure. If not now, then when? If not you, then who? You got this.

# Photos

My first drink south of the border

Hiking... Representing my hometown and home base

One of my very first hikes. December 2017

April 2018, had been hiking twice a week for five months.

I seem to always rep Detroit or Atlanta

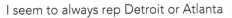

A month before my 1-year anniversary, I led a hike!

My 55th Birthday Party, Super Bowl Sunday 2018.
Forming friendships and finding my tribe.

# Mexico Resources for Moving Abroad:

### Ministry of Foreign Affairs

www.sre.gob.mx

### Mexperience

https://www.mexperience.com

### How Living Abroad Can Reduce Your Stress

www.bestplacesintheworldtoretire.com

### Two Expats Mexico Blog

www.qroo.us, a reliable source of information for people moving to Mexico

Made in the USA
Middletown, DE
21 September 2021